# The Mel Bay Story

By Ray Dankenbring

Mel Bay

Ray Dankenbring

#4 Industrial Drive
Pacific, Missouri 63069
1-800-8-MEL BAY

MEL BAY®

**THE MEL BAY STORY**
Ray Dankenbring



**Mel Bay Publications, Inc.**
Pacific, MO 63069
1-800-8 MEL-BAY



Visit us on the World Wide Web at *http://www.melbay.com*
Send E-mail to us at *email@melbay.com*

ISBN 0-7866-2608-9

Made and printed in the United States of America

# Contents

# PREFACE

*How this book came about...*

In the summer of 1984 my wife and I were on a bus tour in Alaska. We had just left Mt. McKinley and were on our way to Anchorage. The bus made a rest stop at a big restaurant and museum along the way. I was the last person off the bus, and stopped to chat with the driver. He was a school teacher in Anchorage, and drove the tour bus as a summer job.

One thing led to another, and he mentioned that he played guitar. Taking a long shot – or so I thought – I casually asked: "Have you ever heard of Mel Bay?"

His quick answer, which I would hear many times in many parts of the world after that, was: "Sure! I've used his books!"

Now, looking back more than 12 years, I can see that this was a breakthrough for me into the world of Mel Bay. I had known the name Mel Bay since 1961, when we moved to Kirkwood, Missouri, and I began writing and editing for Ralston Purina Company.

I was a "bedroom commuter" – traveling all of the United States and other parts of the world, and coming home to Kirkwood to rest and be with my wife and two sons. Occasionally I would go a few blocks to downtown Kirkwood to the Mel Bay Music Center to buy some new guitar strings, or a pick – I always kept a guitar for fun and relaxation. I had seen Mel Bay a few times, but had never gotten acquainted. Then, in Alaska, the light came on.

When I got back to Kirkwood, I changed my life style. I had taken "early retirement" from the corporate world to go back into full-time writing. I started going to the 10 o'clock Kirkwood Coffee Club, an informal group of men including the mayor, the head of the chamber of commerce, and Kirkwood businessmen. Occasionally Mel Bay would come in and join the group for a few minutes of relaxation and friendly banter. He usually sat quietly listening, but would toss in a joke or two now and then. We slowly got acquainted, and I began to appreciate his quick mind and to learn, bit by bit, pieces of his interesting life and background.

Next, in 1991, my wife and I boarded a cruise ship in San Francisco for a 17-day trip down the coast of Mexico, through the Panama Canal, and finally on to Florida. The big cruise ship had good food, interesting people, and lots of things to do – including nightly entertainment. The featured artist was George Sakellariou, a classical guitarist. He was a native of Greece, but had studied under Andrés Segovia, the world-renowned classical guitarist from Spain. (In 1946 as a student at Iowa State College, I had gone to a campus concert presented by this great musician, Andrés Segovia, and years later attended one of his final concerts in St. Louis.)

My wife and I went to the Sakellariou concerts every night for a week, and thoroughly appreciated this man's talent. George Sakellariou was a fine musician, and a polished gentleman whom we saw often with his wife at a table in our ship's dining room. One night we stopped and introduced ourselves, and complimented him on his performances. I told him about hearing Andrés Segovia on two far-apart occasions. We chatted about that, about Sakellariou's growing up in Greece, and many other things. Finally, again taking a long shot – so I thought – I casually asked: "Have you ever heard of Mel Bay?"

Sakellariou looked at me with his dark, snappy eyes, and in a measured tone said: "Yes – he's the man who writes the books."

That did it! As a writer, I knew there was a story there. (I would later learn that Sakellariou was a member of the Guitar Hall of Fame in Spain. And who else was a member? Mel Bay!) This began an endless chain of meeting people who would respond with nearly the same answer: "Sure – he's the man who writes the books!" I began to feel foolish that I had not known of this man's wide reputation before, but that fits with his pattern of living in Kirkwood – he keeps a low profile. It took me many long months to convince Mel Bay, who is truly modest in many ways, that his life would make a good book.

Meanwhile, I was getting help from others who were telling me the same thing, and eventually Mel and I began talking about it in earnest.

Finally, here is the book – the result of spending many pleasant hours interviewing and just chatting with Mel Bay – in his office, in his home, in my home, at the Kirkwood Coffee Club – wherever I would see him – picking up a steady stream of vignettes and tidbits about his long, interesting, and productive life. We hope that you enjoy reading this book as much as we have enjoyed putting it together.

– Ray Dankenbring

*This is an unusual photo of the informal "Kirkwood Coffee Club" of Kirkwood, Missouri, where Mel Bay lives and operates the Mel Bay Music Center. The photo was the result of a suggestion by Dave Jones, a long-time member, who announced: "Next Friday, everybody wear your cowboy hats!" The members obeyed, and agreed to step outside for this photo. Mel Bay is in the center of the front row, wearing the big Mexican sombrero. At right, in the white coat, is Ray Dankenbring, author of this book. (Photo by Richard N. Thoelke)*

# INTRODUCTION

*A few words from jazz guitar great,*
*Johnny Smith*

Mel Bay is my friend.

Mel once told me: "Wealth is not measured in money or accomplishments; wealth is measured in friends."

Mel Bay is a very wealthy man.

I am a very wealthy man.

Mel Bay is my friend.

Johnny Smith

To one of my very
best friends in the
world: Mel Bay.
Johnny Smith

# The State of Missouri

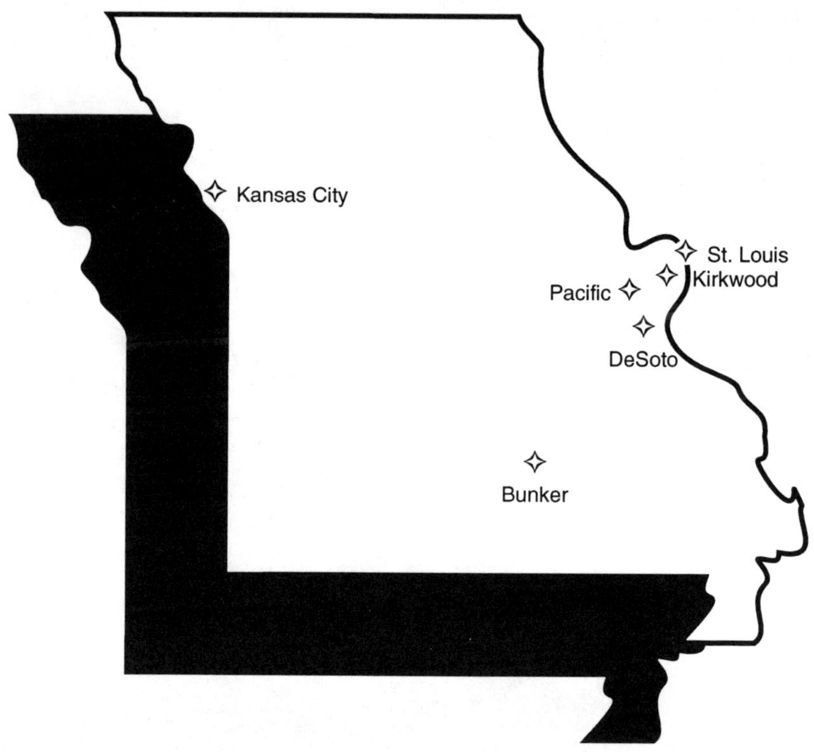


*Missouri is the state in which Mel Bay has spent most of his life. Glancing at this map you can see where he was born (Bunker), lived as a child (St. Louis), grew up (DeSoto), worked as a musician (all across the state, but mostly in St. Louis), started his music store (Kirkwood), and built the Mel Bay Publishing Company plant (Pacific).*

# The Setting

*Here's what the Missouri Hill Country was like when Mel Bay was born*

Mel Bay was born on February 25, 1913, in the small lumber town of Bunker, in the Ozark mountain country of southern Missouri.

If you could look back and see what his world looked like then, what would you see?

By today's standards, life would look pretty rugged and primitive. The first Bay families in America had come from Ireland in the late 1700s, and some years later – 1835 – Mel's great-grandfather had trekked his way back into those rugged, wooded hills of Missouri to settle on some land.

"There were no roads then," Mel Bay relates today. "So my great-grandfather had to follow the creek beds to find his land."

Needless to say, there was no electricity, no telephones, no radio. This was heavy timber country, with many varieties of hardwoods, including oak and hickory, and even a native pine – a big, yellow pine formally called the Shortleaf. The main livelihood for most of the settlers was to cut down the big trees, drag them by horses and mules to a sawmill, cut them into lumber, and haul that lumber out to a shipping point where it could go to help meet a growing demand for building materials.

When Mel's great-grandfather and his family came into this rugged country, the Civil War – the war between the states – was raging on.

Mel relates today: "My people were not concerned about the issues being fought about – they were just trying to make a living."

But there were many ruthless gangs, like those of William Clarke Quantrill (1837 - 1865) who, under the guise of fighting for the Confederate cause, would raid and kill anybody suspected of favoring the Union cause.

One day in 1862 Mel Bay's great-grandmother and her baby boy – who would become Mel's grandfather – were away from the homestead when she heard a lot of shooting. She took her baby boy into a cave in a hillside and hid until the shooting stopped.

When she finally and cautiously approached the homestead, carrying her baby, she was shocked by a horrible sight. The entire family had been killed.

The follow-up to this gruesome prelude to Mel's life was that the gang of men who had done the killing was that of one "Bloody Bill" Anderson, one of Quantrill's guerrilla troops.

This ruthless mob had also wiped out a neighboring family – that of Bill Hildebrand, who survived, and who made it

*Mel and May Bay stand beside the sign marking the cemetery near Bunker, Missouri, where Mel's ancestors – murdered during the Civil War by a guerrilla band – are buried.*

his main goal to track down and eliminate every member of the "Bloody Bill" Anderson gang. Hildebrand succeeded in accomplishing his goal, and satisfied his own sense of justice. He was put on trial for his actions, but a sympathetic jury set him free.

By the time Mel Bay was born in 1913, life was more civilized. The bloody raids by the "bushwhackers," as many settlers called them, were long gone, and the country was in the process of healing and rebuilding. The lumber business in the Bunker area was fading fast as the timber was cut off and hauled away, leaving the hills barren and worthless.

Mel's dad decided it was time to move up to the big city of St. Louis where there would be more opportunity. He got into the grocery business. Then, when Mel was 12 years old, his dad decided to go south of St. Louis 50 miles to the growing town of DeSoto. There he found he could become a real entrepreneur in the growth style of the booming times. He got into the grocery business, the feed business, bought a house, bought land, and even moved into the automobile dealer world. That was the real setting where young Mel began his search for what he wanted to do in life.

The Depression would come along and severely warp his hopes and dreams, but eventually he would struggle and find his niche. It was in 1927, before the stock market crash, when Mel Bay was 14 years old, that he began to find the first clues that he might have a talent for music.

***"My fate had to be music because it was the only thing I could make a buck at."***

**– Mel Bay**

# The Beginning

*How Mel Bay, almost by accident, first discovered that he might like to play a guitar*

"On Christmas day in 1926," recalls today's Mel Bay, "my brother Harlin received a Sears-Roebuck 'Silvertone' guitar ($9.95), and my brother Bill got a ukulele, as presents.

"What did I get? A back-order slip advising me that the violin I was to receive would be delivered within 90 days – long after the Christmas holidays.

"I was disappointed and frustrated, as any young boy would be. I waited and watched my two brothers toying with their new instruments," Mel says.

"It soon became apparent that neither one of them was interested in music, so they gave me the ukulele and the guitar!

"As I look back now over many years of struggle, I can see how little happenings like that can change your life. It certainly changed mine! I started picking around on the guitar and the ukulele. I didn't know what I was doing, but I found that it was fun. I promptly cancelled the violin order and turned my full attention to the two instruments I had in hand.

"While I thought it was fun, I was soon frustrated because I didn't really know how to play anything that sounded good, and I didn't have any books that could show me how to do it right. As I searched around for answers, I turned on our old Atwater-Kent radio and was able to hear Station WSM in Nashville, Tennessee. I began listening to Cid Tanner and his 'Skillet Lickers,' Uncle Dave Macon and Otto Gray, and the Oklahoma Cowboys out of Tulsa.

"That hooked me!

"I got such a yearning to learn how to play that I went to the Hamilton Music Store in DeSoto, where I found two books: *Guckert's Guitar Chords,* and the *Carcassi Classic Guitar Method.*

"I studied and picked, and studied some more and picked some more. I finally managed to form the C, F, G7; the

G, C, D7; and the A, D, E7 chords from the Guckert book. But I didn't know how to use them!

"So then I turned to the *Carcassi Guitar Method* book, published by Theodore Presser back on the East Coast. This book contained excellent playing material for classical guitar. I really wasn't very interested in playing the classic guitar, but it did teach me the *location of the guitar notation.*

"The writer, Matteo Carcassi (1792-1853), was one of the most renowned guitarists of his day, and a prolific composer. His method, studies, and compositions are still widely used in classic guitar teaching.

"As I struggled along trying to figure out how to put things together, I kept searching on my own – playing the different chords that I had learned and trying to put them into some sort of sequence – and looking around for some outside help. I finally stumbled into something unexpected.

"Since there were no modern guitar methods on the market at that time, I was forced to try and locate an instrumental method with *notation similar to the guitar.* As I look back now, this might seem obvious to any good musician. But in my place, and my time, it was like discovering a new world!

"I promptly bought a beginner clarinet method book and, on my guitar, picked my way through it. This was very difficult. I finally decided that I needed some more help – I couldn't really transfer everything I was reading to what I was playing.

"Luckily, I met a man in my dad's grocery store who would help me a lot – a retired band master! I told him about my searching and my problems. He took an interest in me, and agreed to help out. We started getting together for work sessions. He would play the difficult passages on his clarinet, then I would follow him until I was playing it correctly on my guitar.

"Because the guitar is a 'C' instrument, and the clarinet a 'B Flat,' it was impossible for us to play those passages together. But with him playing first, and then me picking it up from there, we were able to make some progress. As I began to learn how to pick out the melodies on my guitar, I got more and more interested and excited.

***"To any young people who want to become proficient with a guitar, or any other instrument, you must discipline yourself to practice.***

***"When I was young and trying to become proficient I would practice for 8 to 10 hours a day.***

***"I'm not saying how many hours a day you have to practice – you can overdo that, too – but I am saying that you have to practice – and practice intelligently."***

**– Mel Bay**

"Again, looking back – I can now see how this led me into a whole lifetime of continuing to learn, adapt, and eventually write my own brand of instruction books. After this experience of adapting methods from the clarinet, I used the knowledge years later when I taught my students from clarinet methods. Duets, trios, and quartets – we put them all together – from clarinet methods.

"(I was relating this evolution to a group of educators one time, and one of them asked me: 'What if a clarinet player wants to join you?' My answer: 'Put a CAPO on the clarinet!')

"I kept working along, adapting everything I could from clarinet methods. I went through every clarinet method I could find. Eventually my efforts started to pay off – I got my first job offer!"

## Starting with Paul Hill

"In 1927, a couple of weeks after I had mastered maybe a dozen chords and was sitting in my dad's grocery store practicing (sometimes when my dad thought I should be doing 'real work'), in through the door walked a man by the name of Paul Hill. He stepped up to the counter to buy something from my dad, then turned around and looked at me, and stood there listening with more than a casual interest. Finally he walked over to me. I stopped playing and looked up at him, wondering what kind of a scolding I might be in for.

"No scolding.

"Instead, he smiled at me, then said: 'So you play the guitar!'

"I bashfully replied: 'Well, no, not very well, but I would like to know how to use these 12 chords I have been working on!'

"He thought for a minute. Then he said: 'Wait here – I'll go get my violin out of the car.'

"Soon he came back into the store, carrying a violin case that looked pretty well scratched and worn, and put it up on the grocery store counter. When he opened it up, my eyes must have glowed, because there was a beautiful, shiny violin. He picked it up, pulled the bow out of the case and tightened the hairs, then drew it across the strings and tuned them carefully.

"I didn't really know what to expect next, but he soon showed me. First he showed me how to apply the correct bass notes with each chord on my guitar. Then, picking up his violin, he played 'Sally Goodin,' very slowly, calling out the chord changes as we went along.

"The more we played, the more excited I got. I thought I was finally learning something! After we finished going through 'Sally Goodin,' he stopped, turned to me and said: 'I think you're beginning to get the idea – want to try another one?'

"'You bet,' I said.

"So we went through 'The Arkansas Traveler,' 'Turkey in the Straw,' 'Flop-eared Mule,' and several other tunes.

"I wasn't following smoothly through every chord change, I must admit. But I discovered that Paul Hill was a patient man – actually a good teacher – and I always remembered that when I was teaching students later.

"Finally he went over, carefully loosened the tension on the bow and put it into the lid of the case, then gently laid the violin in the bottom and closed the lid.

"Before he left he turned to me and said: 'Just keep practicing – maybe we'll play together again sometime.'

"I couldn't have been happier or more inspired to practice and learn. Every spare minute I could find when I didn't have to work in the store and do other chores, I practiced. For two weeks I worked at it – I would hum out those tunes and keep making the chord changes until I had them smoothed out to the point where I really thought I was 'beginning to get the hang of it,' as we said in those days.

"Then Paul Hill came into the store again. He looked at me and asked: 'How are you coming along?'

"I picked up my guitar and ran through my chords.

"He looked at me hard and asked: 'How would you like to play a job?'

"After I had collected my wits I blurted out: 'Yeah!'

"But then I thought to myself – what is a 'job'?

"I soon found out – and I began to learn about the first of many segments of life in the 'outer world' – the first of many I would encounter as I picked my way through the years ahead.

"The 'job' that Paul Hill mentioned was playing in a bootlegging joint, as they were called back in those liquor prohibition days (1920-33). This 'joint' was south of DeSoto, where we lived. It was out in the country. It had two large rooms for square dancing, plus a dining room.

"A square dance 'set' would get ready in one room where we played – and played – until they gave out from sheer fatigue. While they (and we) were racing along through many dances and many tunes, another group would get set up in the other room. So then we would move into the other room and play while they (and we) wore themselves to a frazzle!

"This went on until one o'clock in the morning! For a young boy just starting out, it was a new, long, hard experience.

"I thought I was accustomed to working hard around my dad's store, but pressing down on those strings and strumming a guitar for hour after hour was something new – and tough. My fingers were not calloused enough for such a marathon, and by midnight the neck of my guitar was actually covered with blood from my bleeding fingers.

"The following week Paul Hill asked me to play another job.

"I didn't want to go through another night of bleeding fingers – and they wouldn't be healed and toughened by then, as they would be years later. I took a small, three-cornered file and deepened the string grooves in the nut at the head of the fingerboard on my guitar.Then I put the strings back on, tuned it, and tried playing.

“That helped! It took less pressure to hold the strings down, since they were closer to the frets. Hopefully now my sore fingers could make it through the night.

“My fingers did survive – and I survived. They (and I) both got tougher and tougher as we played for just about every bootlegging joint in the area.

“Looking back, that really was the start of my ‘professional career’!

“But it would end soon. When my parents found out that I was not ‘playing for church activities,’ they made me quit.

“It was a good beginning experience. I would learn to pick out the good things from it and to avoid the bad – like bootleg moonshine.

## Playing with Oscar Gibbons

“On another day when I was stealing a few minutes from working in the store, and practicing on my guitar, another man walked in who would add to my experiences. His name was Oscar Gibbons. He walked up to me and told me that he played the mandolin, and suggested that we get together and play some tunes.

“That turned out to be great fun.

“We got good enough that we were asked to play for an assembly program at the DeSoto High School – our first public appearance!

“Our first selection was ‘The Wreck of the Old 97.’

When we finished, the applause was terrific! We quickly followed that with 'Yes, Sir, That's My Baby,' 'Springtime in the Rockies,' 'Red Wing,' and a few others we knew. We had a hard time quitting – the school audience loved our music!

"That really spurred us on to practice and learn more pieces, and from that time on, we were invited back to play at many school activities – assemblies, parties, meetings."

## My First Good Guitar – "The National Triolian"

*Mel Bay with his National Triolian guitar.*

"During the hot summer of 1928, between my freshman and sophomore years in the DeSoto high school, I worked in a shoe factory. For shoving racks of shoes from the finishing department to the shipping department, I was paid $9.00 a week.

"I saved all of the money I could, and at the end of the summer I had $50 in my pocket. I had put it there for the purpose of going into a music store in St. Louis and buying myself a better guitar than the old Silvertone I had been playing.

"One store refused to sell me a guitar because I was only 16 years old.

"Another store operator asked me: 'Boy, where did you get that money?'

"That really burned me, so I told him: 'It's none of your damn business – I earned it!' And then I walked out.

"Finally I went to the Ludwig Music House. There Mr. Ruester showed me a new type of guitar that he had just received. I played it, and immediately fell in love with it. It was named 'The National Triolian,' and the price on it was $65.00.

"I told Mr. Ruester that I only had fifty dollars with me, but I would like to put that down, and then go home and get the rest. I told him that I had to go down to DeSoto for the balance.

"He said: 'You mean that you would go all the way to DeSoto (a hard trip in those days) and bring the rest of the money back to me?'

"I told him that I would.

"He said: 'Son, give me the fifty dollars and take this guitar back to DeSoto with you.'

"I never forgot that great act of kindness, understanding, and helpfulness to a young man, and during the rest of my life I have tried to remember that whenever I am dealing with young people.

*"A footnote: Along the way I traded that guitar in for a better one, and on through the years I have owned and played many guitars, as most professionals do. If I had kept that Triolian (hindsight), it would bring about $10,000 on the*

*vintage market. But such are the fortunes – or misfortunes – of life."*

## Next, Mel tries the tenor banjo

"I wanted to play in a dance band, but the unamplified guitar of those days was simply too soft for a rhythm instrument in a loud, brassy, jazz band. The tenor banjo was ideal for that purpose, so I decided to take up that instrument. I bought a Gibson Mastertone and developed a chordal technique playing melody and rhythm.

"Our little six-piece group in DeSoto became the most popular band in that area, every weekend playing in the popular dance halls. This was still during prohibition time – before 1932 when Franklin D. Roosevelt was elected and changed the law that prohibited liquor. At the dances where we played, the bootleggers kept the dancers well supplied with 'joy juice.'

"Once in awhile I would have to say to the boys: 'It's beginning to look rough tonight – so let's close this thing early.'

"And how would I do that?

"I would simply call out in a loud voice: 'Tag Dance!'

"That meant that any man in the room could go up to any couple on the dance floor, tag the guy and say that he was going to dance with his girl. Well, not every guy wanted that to happen, and soon the fights were on! *What fights we saw!*

"Finally the owner of the joint would say: 'Okay, boys, play "Home Sweet Home" before they wreck the joint!' So we would play 'Home Sweet Home,' which meant that the dance was over."

## Playing for Dr. Binks' Medicine Shows

"I really liked playing the tenor banjo (and also the guitar, of course), and kept working away at it. I played the technical and novelty arrangements of Harry Reser, Ralph Collichio, and Roy Smeck to add to my repertoire. That got me some guest solo appearances on the radio, and I was still only 16.

"In the back of my father's store one day, while sitting on a sack of potatoes playing my tenor banjo, a man walked back and said: 'You play a mighty fine banjo!'

"I thanked him for the compliment.

"Then he introduced himself as Mr. Barkus, and said: 'I could use a good banjo player for my medicine show!'

"He offered me $5.00 a night to play for him. That was *good money* in those days, for a young guy like me. It turned out that Mr. Barkus sold a 'medicine' called 'Dr. Binks' Eagle Herb Tonic,' which I will explain in a minute. I lived at home, but we would drive to nearby towns to set up the big medicine show.

"Mr. Barkus owned a Rickenbacker automobile, one of the first autos with four-wheel brakes and a safety-glass windshield. Up on front of the radiator he had mounted a pair of Texas longhorns.

"When we were ready to start the show, my job was to crawl up, sit on a pillow on the radiator, in the middle of those big longhorns, and play my banjo. But first – Mr. Barkus had to make sure that he had an adequate supply of the Eagle Herb Tonic.

"So the first thing he did when arriving in a new town would be to locate the local bootlegger to obtain the proper ingredients for his elixir.

"It was properly named 'Eagle' Herb Tonic, because after a few swigs of that stuff a man would forget all of his aches and pains and feel that he could fly like an eagle!

"But before selling any of his magic medicine, Mr. Barkus did one other thing. He would find a local yokel who would agree to testify that the tapeworm in the jar (which Barkus carried with him from town to town) was from that yokel who had taken some of this marvelous Eagle Herb Tonic! Then he was ready to really bring in the business, and I would keep playing away at my banjo to attract more of a crowd.

"The crowd actually fell for Barkus' line of chatter and bought that wonderful Dr. Binks' Eagle Herb Tonic.

"I played along with this game for three weeks – always playing the banjo to attract a crowd.

"Then I decided 'enough is enough,' and left the show.

"But I did learn another valuable lesson: *Music and salesmanship* – put them together – they are winners!"

# Mel meets the Great Roy Smeck

"Roy Smeck was the 'Wizard of the Strings.' He made many records featuring the Hawaiian guitar, ukulele, guitar, and tenor banjo. I had many of his books and records. He, like Harry Reser and Nick Lucas, was a great inspiration to me.

"In 1928 Roy Smeck was appearing at the Ambassador Theatre in St. Louis in a show highlighting Ed Lowry and Ginger Rogers. I drove up from DeSoto to see and hear his great performance. After the performance, which absolutely enthralled me, I asked one of the ushers if I could meet Mr. Smeck.

"The usher flatly refused to let me see him.

"Then I asked him, politely, if he could ask Roy Smeck to autograph a couple of his tenor banjo solo folios that I had brought with me. I waited nervously. Finally the usher came back and said to me: 'Roy would like to meet you.'

"I could hardly contain myself. I bashfully walked back and was warmly greeted by the great Roy Smeck!

"That was a real inspiration and booster for me – a green, 16-year-old youth getting the chance to actually meet such a great man. Not only did Roy Smeck sign my folios, he had the usher seat me in the very first row for another performance! I returned home on Cloud Nine.

"Approximately 25 years later I did a solo performance for an American Guild of Music Convention in Cincinnati, Ohio. Roy Smeck was the final performance. I heard that his guitarist didn't show up and that he was in trouble – he needed a backup man. So I volunteered to do it for him.

"He said: 'But we haven't ever played together – how can we make this work?'

"I simply said: 'You go ahead – I'll follow.' And I did.

"He was amazed at the fact that I accompanied him so well without a rehearsal. It was a thrill for me to be able to do so – and to be on the same stage with one of my idols.

"I accompanied Roy Smeck many times after that. Those times were among some of the most pleasurable musical experiences, and we developed a lifelong friendship."

*Young Roy Smeck befriended young Mel Bay – years later they would perform together* *(see FRIENDS chapter).*

*Mel and Roy Smeck circa 1960.*

# Eddie Lang – one of Mel Bay's early idols

As a young kid, Mel Bay was entranced when he could turn on his dad's old Atwater-Kent radio – with the big horn speaker – and hear the great guitar of Eddie Lang.

Eddie Lang (1904-1933) was an Italian from Philadelphia who expanded the harmonic horizons of the guitar far beyond what most guitarists of that era were playing. He developed his own single-string ad lib solo style that was probably 10 years ahead of its time. Lang's guitar was heard as an outstanding accompaniment, or as a solo, or as part of a duet with violinist Joe Venuti.

*Eddie Lang*
*Photo courtesy Duncan P. Schiedt*

Eddie Lang died just as the electric guitar was being born, so he never participated in that new sound – but he made his own sound that was heard before the first amplifier was ever plugged in.

Some of Eddie Lang's finest solos and duets can be found in the Mel Bay book entitled *Masters of the Plectrum Guitar.*

# 1931

## *Wiped out by the Depression*

Mel kept practicing and playing in many different jobs as he continued on in high school in 1929.

"I spent every spare minute of my time practicing, probing, and searching for ideas and material from musicians, teachers, and anything in published form," he says.

"During the summer of 1929 I went with Jim Roach's Hawaiian group, at that time a very popular group – playing supper clubs and shows."

Despite his musical talents and success, Mel had in mind that he ought to go to college and get an 'acceptable' degree – like in engineering. And he had saved his money to do just that.

He says: "In 1931, upon graduation from high school in DeSoto, Missouri, I started to enroll at Rolla School of Mines in Missouri, to study engineering."

But the big stock market crash which had hit Wall Street in 1929 was washing like a giant tidal wave across the entire country – including DeSoto, Missouri.

Says Mel, still with some sadness: "I had $3,000 in the bank – that was a lot of money in those days, and I had worked hard day and night for several years saving it in pennies, nickels, quarters, and dollars. Before I could draw my money out of the bank – the bank closed. I was wiped out, financially and mentally. Not only was I wiped out, but my hard-working father suffered a huge loss through stock crash losses, depreciated land values, and then the bank crash.

"This was the lowest point in my whole life," says Mel. "My father was the greatest man I ever met. If I wore stilts, I could barely reach his ankles.

"His sense of humor was classic," – and Mel constantly shows that he inherited that talent. But a sense of humor wasn't enough to cope with the horrendous devastation of this financial wipeout. It took more than that. It took faith, hope, courage – anything a person could muster – which Mel's father did.

Mel relates: "He gathered us around the family table and said: 'We have lost our gas and oil distributorship, our Chrysler-Plymouth agency, our home and money, but we still have the most important things in life: We have our grocery store, we have each other, we have our health, and we have faith in the Good Lord and the knowledge that he will surely look over us through these troubled times.'"

*Mel's parents – Albert and Edith Bay*

# Out of the Doldrums

## *Mel starts again*

Reflecting back to those dismal Depression days, Mel relates: "I was sitting in front of my father's store, head drooped down in a sorrowful mood, feeling low and depressed. No job, no college, and very few friends, I was telling myself.

"Reverend Wilson, the Presbyterian minister, walked by, stopped, and said: 'Boy, you look like you lost your last friend!'"

Mel says he replied: "Yes – about three thousand of them – all dollars."

The minister thought for a moment, then in a firm voice said: "Mel, the Lord has given you a great talent in music. So stick with it and I'm sure that something great will be in store for you!"

"Starting the next day, I began practicing eight hours a day," Mel says.

"Later on my father, seeing me putting forth a lot of effort, enrolled me in the Hugo School of Music in St. Louis where I was under the tutelage of Bunny Longo. Bunny was the

*Bunny Longo was Mel's music tutor at the Hugo School of Music in St. Louis, Missouri.*

finest banjoist in the St. Louis area – one of the finest technicians ever to teach and perform. She featured me in many recitals and radio programs during the two years that I studied under her.

"In 1935 Bunny Longo asked me to take over her class, since she was going to get married." That was the beginning of a great teaching career.

"But it wasn't all roses," Mel quickly adds.

"I moved my meager belongings to St. Louis, into the attic of a boarding house with no heat, no air conditioning, not even a fan. In the winter my job was to get up at 5 a.m. and stoke the furnace and sweep the floors for the 'privilege' of staying there. I slept on a couch.

"In the summer it was too hot to sleep in the attic, so I would go out to Forest Park and sleep on the ground, just hoping to get some air. To earn money for food, I played in taverns for tips – usually pennies and nickels. Before taking over the students, Bill Hugo advised me that I would have to teach each student five lessons for free before I would receive the 50 percent commission on each student.

## There was a positive side!

Says Mel: "On the positive side, heading up the fretted instrument staff at Hugo was a terrific experience because I became associated with the finest musicians in St. Louis, and my music was being featured regularly on Radio Station KWK when it was a prime station under the late Thomas Patrick Convey.

"After I had finished giving my five free music lessons, teaching tenor banjo, I started earning some money by teaching for Hugo. But I was still playing in taverns and joints for food money.

"My diet consisted of a donut and coffee for 10 cents for breakfast, a nickel bag of peanuts for lunch, and usually six White Castle hamburgers for supper, at a cost of 25 cents. I was surviving, but I wanted to move on, so in 1935 I decided to open my own studio at the Gravois Music Center in south St. Louis.

"Bill Hugo told me that I could not take the students to my new place.

"I told him that I had bought them with those free lessons, so if he wanted trouble over that matter, I was ready.

"He backed off.

"As I began giving lessons at the Gravois Music Center, one day a very beautiful and talented young lady by the name of May Gebelein came in to begin lessons.

"As I began giving her lessons and getting acquainted with her, something besides music from guitars became evident. I was more and more impressed by her charm and personality – as well as her musicianship. A year after the lessons began, we were married. *(See Vignettes for a lighter side of this romance.)*

"We actually dated for only six weeks before getting married, but looking back I can see that the relationship started the minute she came through door – and it has been going for 60 years!"

Giving his remarkable wife some credit for the success of the Bay businesses later, Mel says: "It was May who would be given the job of raising our two children during the many years I would be traveling the entire United States and Canada to sell my instruction book."

*May Gebelein, when she was a guitar student of Mel's*

Mel and May's two children are William Bay and Susan (Bay) Banks.

"And it would be May who would later run the retail store business as I continued to develop the music publishing end."

Looking back at his times at the Gravois Music Center, Mel says: For years my routine was as follows: I would work all day at the Gravois Music Center, starting in the morning by preparing lessons, then teaching all day. Then I would play a gig at night with my trio (piano, bass, and guitar). And then, in the wee hours, I would pack orders for my books down in the basement of our house. May would make sure that the packages got to the post office."

*Mel and May Bay on their 50th anniversary.*

# RADIO, THE BIG BANDS, AND MEL BAY

*They grew up together*

Mel Bay was born in 1913. Little did he know until some years later that two other "births" at about the same time would come into his life and intertwine with him for many years. Those two "births" were radio, and the big bands.

Both were in their infancy in the early 1900s, as was Mel, and all three would have a lot of growing and learning to do – but they would do a lot in the next 25 to 30 years.

The "big bands" didn't just start as such, all at once. They had to grow from small groups – usually a violin, piano, drums, and banjo. This growth started around 1910.

The interest in dancing grew, and that forced the slow and steady growth of the small groups into bigger groups, and eventually into the big bands. By the time young Mel Bay was beginning to walk, there was evidence that in some of the big cities – a "million miles away" from tiny Bunker, Missouri where Mel still lived – both radio and bands were beginning to take some steps and grow.

In 1911 Wilbur Sweatman had a group playing in Chicago. A few years later a man started playing in Los Angeles and would become almost a household name – Paul Whiteman.

These were followed by a sprinkling, or maybe we should say a steady shower, of names to be heard from as Mel Bay would get into the music business...Ted Lewis, Abe Lyman, Charlie Edgar, and Loring "Red" Nichols. Small groups began adding trombones, trumpets, another banjo, then violins and bass...

In 1916 Pennsylvania native Fred Waring launched his first venture – a six-man string group which eventually would grow into the big band called Fred Waring and his Pennsylvanians.

There were many others, including Jan Garber, who came out of World War I (which ended in 1918) to organize a four-piece dance orchestra – which would grow into a full-size, well-known dance band.

# 1920s – starting to boom

The First World War was over, and as seems to happen after any war ends (including World War II in 1946), people were ready to celebrate. Dancing flourished in the 1920s, and with it more new bands – Lawrence Welk, a native of North Dakota; "The Scranton Sirens" out East, which had some new players named Russ Morgan on trombone and Jimmy Dorsey on saxophone.

In 1925 a group headed by Ben Pollack included sidemen Glenn Miller and Benny Goodman, and the California Collegians hired a young musician named Fred MacMurray, who would show up in movies a few years later.

From North Carolina came Kay Kyser, who would become a big name. Many other new names that would later

*The "Bay Big Band Tradition" continued with a band fronted by Mel's teenage son Bill (circa 1960). Bill is on lead trumpet. The alto sax player on the right is David Sanborn.*

become well known were just getting their start in the "roaring twenties" – Ted Weems, Vincent Lopez, Duke Ellington, Wayne King, Guy Lombardo, and Louie Armstrong.

## Radio was spreading

Radio stations were popping up across the continent in the 1920s. The networks were not formed yet, but they would soon be in the making.

Also in the making was a young man in DeSoto, Missouri. His family had moved from the small Ozark town of Bunker up to big St. Louis when he was only a year old; then had moved 50 miles south to the town of DeSoto when he was 12. In just two more years he would pick up his first guitar and start picking away – never to stop. That young man was Mel Bay.

# The Guitar Keeps Evolving, and Changing

*A brief history of the instrument*

It is believed that the first guitars were made in Spain, with a flat top and a round hole in the center of the sound body. Immigrants to the United States brought guitars (and other instruments) with them, and eventually the guitar was spread across the new country.

The guitar was used mostly for home enjoyment rather than as a public concert instrument. But as the country developed, as radio and bands began to form in the early 1900s, the guitar began emerging from its humble position into a new aura of recognition.

In the 1920s and '30s there were several manufacturers in the United States – Gibson, Martin, Epiphone, and others.

A new model with an arched face, thus called the "arch top," was developed. It had the "f" holes with a "chunky" sound that would project out across a crowd on a dance floor. At the same time there was the steel guitar with a round hole, and it

***"Music is such an incredibly diverse field and the guitar is the most diverse of all. You find guitarists who love flamenco, classical, contemporary classic, Celtic, 18th-19th century, early music, steel-string guitar, folk, country, bluegrass, renaissance, cajun, blues, rock, plus a few new ones coming along – the interest seems endless."***

**– William Bay**

was considered the main instrument of country people who played for fun, and for events like square dances and socials.

Says William Bay: "The old-style guitars played by greats such as Eddie Lang and Carl Kress produced an unusual phenomena – incredibly *strong left hands* that could play chord solos with great speed."

When one single note on a string did nothing – when it was drowned out by the noise of the crowd – the power of the heavy chord would carry over and could be heard. Thus, if guitarists of those times wanted to be heard, they simply had to develop great chord solo techniques.

## The development of the electric guitar

George Barnes, a top guitarist in the United States from the late '30s up until his death in 1977, said: "In 1931 my older brother, who was an electronic genius, built me a pickup and an amplifier before they were even out on the market. He did this for me because he knew I wanted to play solo lines which could be heard in a band."

That could have been among the first experiments with the electric amplifiers now so common around the world.

There is some question about who actually produced the first commercial electric guitar. Some music history books say that National Dobro came out with the first model in 1932.

As this book is written, there is an exhibition at the National Museum of American History in Washington, D.C. that shows electric guitars "From Frying Pan to Flying V." It shows the "Rickenbacker Frying Pan," a long-necked guitar with a small body (maybe 12 inches in diameter) that does look like a frying pan, with electrical outlet for the amplifier.

The "Gibson Flying V" in the exhibit does have an inverted V-shaped body that flares out from the end of the neck like two legs, built in 1957.

From this beginning there was almost an explosion of electrical, and finally electronic attachments that have boomed guitar sounds out over any kind of other noises that might otherwise interfere with hearing them.

Not all guitarists, including Mel Bay, fully appreciate the magnitude of some of those amplifications. "But they are part of today's world," Mel says with a grin, "and they mean a lot of business for us."

Soon the world of guitars became the world of the "plugged" and the "unplugged."

The "unplugged" – the unamplified guitars – continued to be popular and models continued to be produced by Martin, Gibson, D'Angelico, and others. The popular acoustic guitars with the round holes continued to be the Gibson, Martin (developed in the 1800s), and the Washburn.

# What ever happened to the "plectrum"?

"Plectrum," which means "pick," was a common term in the guitar world at one time, but today the term is rarely used. Instead, people refer to such a guitar as a "flat pick" or "flatted."

The "f" hole jazz guitars are still referred to as "arch tops," due to their rounded, curved face.

***"Fifty years ago the guitar was for hillbilly pickers and a few classical players with a limited audience. I've seen this instrument become the bulwark of the music industry. It's grown beyond my greatest expectations, and I don't see anything on the horizon that's going to replace it. What would you have?***

***"With the guitar, you've got an instrument that plays all types of music, and you've got one that anybody can afford, and you can't name a facet of society it won't adapt itself to."***

**– Mel Bay**

# The Mel Bay D'Angelico Guitar

*How the Mel Bay Model came about*

"The 'Stradivarius' of the guitar makers, in my opinion, was John D'Angelico of New York," says Mel Bay.

"He produced four styles: the A, the B, the Excel, and the New Yorker. In the late '40s, he dropped the A and B, and in the mid-'50s he introduced the Mel Bay model. Here's how that came about," recalls Mel.

"I had played D'Angelico since 1935. I had an Excel for my solo work and a New Yorker for my rhythm work. After the war I talked to John and said I'd like to have him make me a guitar with a New Yorker cutaway body and an Excel-type neck, because of my small hands – and a little heavier head-stock for balance," Mel says.

"John made that guitar for me, and I still have it. I think that it could be the first one of that particular line. Everybody who saw that guitar liked it and asked Johnny to make one like it. He named it *The Mel Bay Model.* I was quite honored that

*Mel's original D'Angelico "Mel Bay Model"*

John would name it after me," Mel says with a smile.

"The increase in value of this line of instruments has been incredible," Mel says.

"They began at several hundred dollars, and today are in the tens of thousands. My guitar has been appraised at over $100,000," Mel says, shaking his head.

*Mel's original D'Angelico "Mel Bay Model"*

*Here, young Mel Bay plays an early-model D'Angelico guitar in the 1930s. In the 1940s he would have John D'Angelico make a model to his specifications, with a thinner neck and cutaway body (shown on previous pages).*

# THE SEARCHING YEARS...

*The struggling years...*
*The growing years...*
*and several careers!*

To cover many of the details of the years of Mel Bay's life between the ages of 20 and 70 – a span of 50 busy years – would take several volumes.

But as Mel himself says: "People don't want to read volumes. They don't want to read every detail. Try to sort out what is significant and what will be interesting to read!"

This short chapter is a quick overview of that period.

A few general statements can be made that will set the basis of Mel's life during that important span of years.

One is that he was full of energy, drive, and a desire to overcome the sting of the Depression and to make his way in the world. All of his friends attest to the fact that "he gave it his best shot." He didn't eat or drink much, and he didn't seem to need much sleep. He seemed to thrive on work – and work he did!

What kind of work? He did so many things that you could write a long list of separate "careers."

He played professionally for bands that came to St. Louis – he was the Number One guitar and banjo artist on everybody's list, and he was booked as far as a year in advance for jobs.

He continued to teach students – as many as 100 a week.

He traveled, both for playing jobs, and to sell and establish markets for his books.

Meanwhile, he and May had the retail store, and in the 1940s their two children, Susan and William, were born.

May Bay, devoted and hard-working like her striving husband, was often left alone to raise the two children and keep the guitar method instruction book sales moving. She, too, led several careers – housewife, mother, retailer, and store manager, to cite just four.

Both Mel and May Bay had common goals – to survive, to succeed, and to accomplish...and to raise good children.

Add one more factor to all of their attributes – both had real musical talent, and they passed that along to their two children and six grandsons, all of whom inherited both musical talent and the will to work hard.

"As we look back over the hard, struggling years, we don't look at the negative things – we look at the positive," say both Mel and May Bay.

"When we do that, we feel that we were repaid for our efforts, and are blessed with a wonderful family, which gives us the most satisfaction of anything we have achieved."

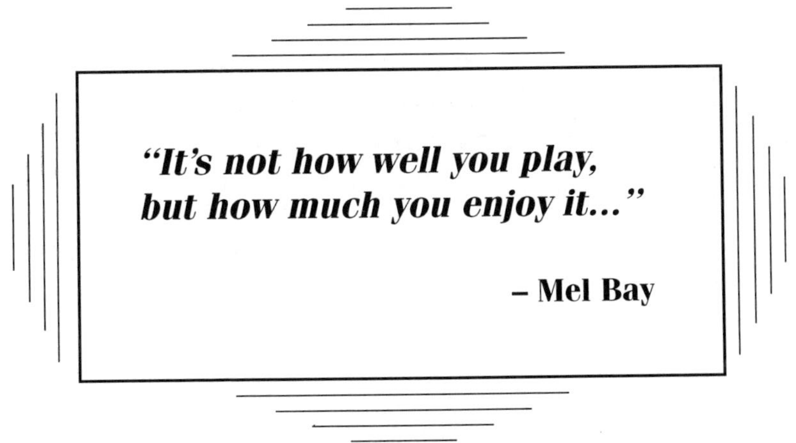

***"I looked up every guitar teacher in the United States. They all told me the same thing – this is what they'd been looking for. We began selling directly to them. I'd come home after a hard day's work, pack books and ship them off.***

***"I decided to increase distribution so I went around the country again, this time visiting music dealers.***

***"I showed them I had all the teachers buying from me and said I'd like to channel these customers to them. Then when I had enough dealers, I went to the jobbers and told them I'd like to channel the dealers to them. It's the first time in the publishing, business to my knowledge, that anyone started in this direction."***

**– Mel Bay**

*Young Mel Bay dressed up to play at a social event or with a big band.*

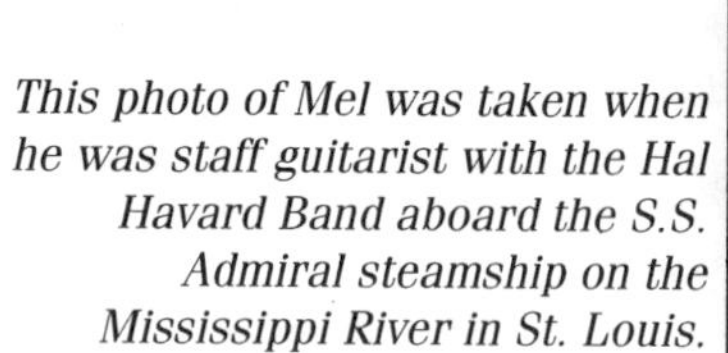

*This photo of Mel was taken when he was staff guitarist with the Hal Havard Band aboard the S.S. Admiral steamship on the Mississippi River in St. Louis.*

*Young Mel Bay became proficient on both the guitar and banjo, and played either – depending on requirements of the "job," "gig," or big band.*

*Laura and Claudia Jones, daughters of David Jones, publisher, historian and long-time citizen of Kirkwood, Missouri, get special attention from Mel Bay at Kirkwood High School in the 1960s.*

*For many years Mel Bay was a top guitar professional in St. Louis, in constant demand by the big bands that came in, and as a backup musician for many vocalists.*

*Guitar great Al Valenti made a special performance at the Webster Groves, Missouri, high school in 1949. Here he is shown with Mel Bay at left and Hans Lemcke, head of the music department at the school. Mel published some of Al's solos in his book* Masters of the Plectrum Guitar.

*Jimmy Caldwell (above right), manager of the Music Department of the St. Louis Music Supply Company, buys the first guitar method book from Mel Bay in 1947. They sold well, and he bought many hundreds to meet the demand.*

*This is the cover of the first Mel Bay guitar method book written and published in 1948 (above). Millions of copies can be found in the hands of guitar players of all creeds and colors around the world. His* Orchestral Chord System *was published in 1947.*

> ***"He wrote a chord book and developed some of his own guitar methods because he wasn't pleased with what was then available.***
>
> ***"He started writing the first of eight books in 1947, then he started criss-crossing the country from then until about 1959.***
>
> ***"He went to New York and just about everywhere with his book and guitar methods, trying to find a market for them, but at that time there just wasn't any."***
>
> **– William Bay**

*Mel Bay visits a music dealer in Fairbanks, Alaska in the 1960s, which happened to be at a time of a serious flood, as evidenced by the water in the foreground.*

*Mel Bay taught as many as 100 students per week from his guitar method books, while at the same time traveling, playing gigs, and helping his wife, May, operate the retail business.*

*David Gornston (above right), one of the great writers and publishers of woodwind method books, visits with Mel Bay at the Ludwig School of Music in the 1950s. He was interested in the fact that Mel Bay had picked up clarinet music to apply to his guitar methods. Below: One of Mel Bay's satisfactions was the opportunity to teach his guitar methods to young students, such as this class in a Missouri high school.*

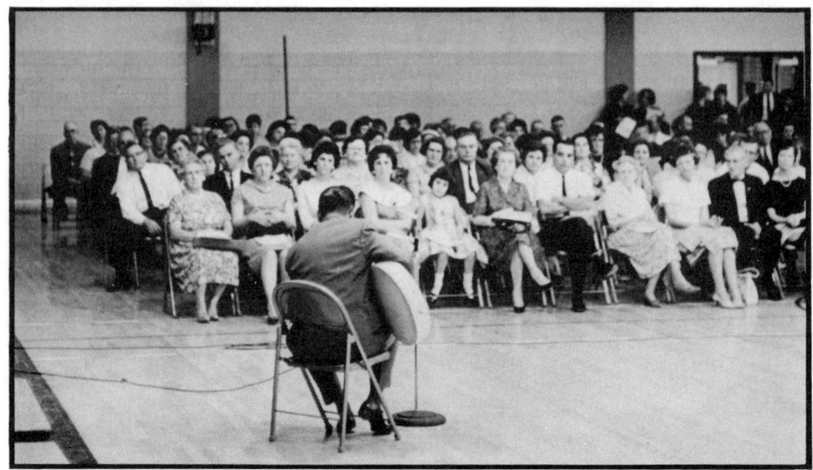

*Performing and instructing at hundreds of seminars and classes in schools, Mel Bay made a lasting imprint on the minds of thousands of stringed instrument students and music educators.*

***"It has been my goal to elevate and expand the range of music available for the guitar and to create a system of instruction which nurtures and develops truly great musicians."***

**– Mel Bay**

# Breaking Away

*...from "Playing Everywhere, Every Night"*

In 1957, after many years of traveling the entire United States, playing with bands in smoke-filled, noisy ballrooms, hotels, night clubs, theatres...staying in crummy hotel rooms, eating at irregular hours...Mel Bay decided that it was time to change his life.

He says: "I decided that if I kept this up for the rest of my life, away from family, and home, keeping up the treadmill pace, that I would end up like many of my good friends – in bad health, maybe *poor* again, and maybe dead. So, finally, I got smart enough to conclude that 30 years of that was enough. I decided to make the break – go back home, put my time and efforts into publishing, retailing, and getting acquainted with my family.

## Johnny Smith had made the break

Mel Bay's good friend Johnny Smith, rated as one of the top jazz guitarists in the United States, had reached a similar conclusion at about the same time. Smith was on a fast track in New York City.

He had shown his incredible guitar magic with the NBC orchestra under Arturo Toscanini, sat in with the New York Philharmonic, played in legendary nightclubs on 52nd Street, made more than 30 albums of his own, and spent endless hours with guitar in hand. He rarely saw his wife and three young children as a "regular husband and father."

In 1958 Smith's wife died, leaving him with the children to raise. Smith knew that he had to make a break with his rat-race schedule. He had to change his life.

Smith's mother and two brothers lived in Colorado Springs, Colorado. He sent his children out to live with them while he tied up things in New York.

Then he moved.

Smith commuted to New York occasionally to do some playing jobs, and he played in Denver's Melody Lounge. But his interest in the traveling jobs was fading.

He had designed a new instrument for The Gibson Guitar Company, and his friends there helped him and his new wife Sandy start their own music store in Colorado Springs. Then he bought some acreage up in the Rocky Mountains, and eventually his friend Mel bought some property from him.

This led to many happy fishing hours on a lake, and relaxing get-togethers for the two music men with their families and friends.

"Moving out here was one of the few intelligent things I've done in my life," Smith says, with his usual modesty about his own abilities.

Then he adds: "As a traveling musician, you have to wait in airports, the food is bad in some places, and you never know what kind of musicians you have to play with. To get on the stage and play with bad ones can be the most miserable, degrading thing in the world. That lifestyle may be glamorous when you're young, but not when you get older."

Mel Bay certainly agrees with his friend on that.

*Mel and May Bay with their daughter Susan and their son Bill at their 50th wedding anniversary.*

> ***"I consider myself a happy man. I have a wonderful family and probably the most wonderful wife a man could ever have."***
>
> **– Mel Bay**

*Mel Bay holds his grandson Kevin at a family reunion. Mel's father is second from right. His daughter Sue is on the left.*

*Mel's grandson Matt posing for an ad shot.*

*Mel and May on one of their many trips overseas.*

*William A. (Bill) Bay and his father, Mel Bay, stand in front of their publishing plant (above) located at Pacific, Missouri, a small town about 25 miles west of Kirkwood, home of the Mel Bay Music Center. It was a cold day in 1978!*

*Colorado, a favorite retreat for Mel and his busy family, provides some quiet time for reflection about trends in the music business.*

*Mel, Bill and grandson Matthew posed for a catalog shot. Bill's dog wandered into the picture seemingly to "protect Matthew from the photographer."*

*This is the Mel Bay Music Center (above) on West Jefferson Avenue in Kirkwood, Missouri, a suburb of St. Louis. Mel and May Bay opened this center in 1952 and have expanded it several times. This is a stopping place for customers and musicians from around the world.*

*Mel gives a special performance to the Kirkwood Coffee Club, under the weight of his heavy Mexican sombrero. (photo by author)*

*Mel posing with son Bill and all six grandsons (he has no granddaughters!) for an ad shot.*

# *Three generations of Bays performing!*

*Mel, Bill, and 11-year-old grandson Collin performing at the publishing plant for the "1996 Christmas Dock Door Concert."*

*A recent shot of Mel and May taken on a cruise.*

***"For guitar methods, he's one of the grand old men of the music industry.***

***"There's not a print music store anywhere that hasn't sold a Mel Bay book.***

***"It's very rare for one book – Guitar Method 1 – to have such a long shelf life. It's definitely got to be one of the all-time best sellers for any kind of book."***

**– Madeleine Crouch**
**Retail Print Music Dealers Association**
**Dallas, Texas**

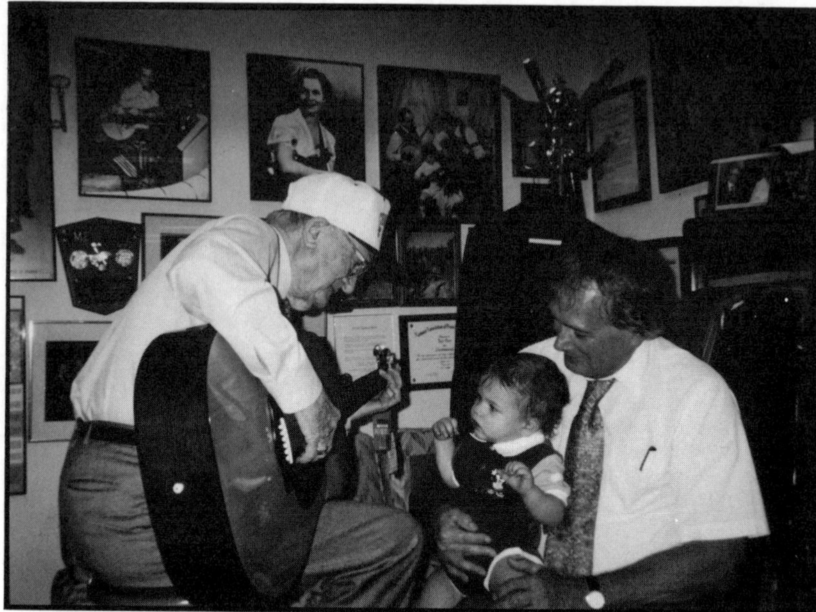

*A fascination for the guitar and its sounds is passed along from Mel Bay to young Alex Muenster and his proud grandpa Bob Brinkman while Mel played "Happy Birthday" to Alex for his first.*

***Writing for* Guitar Player *magazine in 1978, Don Menu said: "Mel Bay became known as the* only guitarist *in the vicinity of St. Louis who could read or handle any real solo work in a band."***

# As Times Were Changing

*– Mel kept up with them*

In 1959, as Mel was picking and writing and teaching his way into the ever-expanding world of guitar music, he wrote this for various trade magazines:

"For the past 30 years the guitar has been my way of life, and I might say it has been a very enjoyable one. The instrument (guitar) has really adapted itself to the American way of life since we have become a nation of travelers, and the hope is now the center of entertainment. Now, with shorter working hours, the people have more time for that sort of thing. I always think of the capital letter 'G.' The letter 'G' stands for *guitar, groups, gatherings,* and *gaiety!*

"How can we account for its popularity?

"I think for the answer we have to go back a long way. Number one, the instrument has always been rich in heritage. In fact, the history of America could be a chronicle of the guitar. It was played in Colonial America. It was found in the cabins of the earliest settlers. It accompanied the pioneers on the westward trek, where upon their arrival in the Far West they found that for two hundred years it had been the household instrument of the Spanish-speaking West.

"People buy guitars, I think, because there are no barriers to playing the instrument. There are no geographical or social barriers from Park Avenue across to Arizona, from the shacks of the southern states to the log camps of the lumberjacks in the Northwest.

"There are no physical or mental barriers. The instrument is light, compact, easily handled, and it can accompany the ambitious performer into the uppermost realms of serious music. There are no gender barriers as it is equally popular with both sexes.

"And finally, there are no age barriers. When the young hopeful dons his first cowboy outfit his little Gene Autry guitar completes his regalia. When he outgrows the cowboy suit and grows into his first blue jeans, his guitar is most important as he is now a rock teenager, and we all know the importance of the instrument to that generation. When he leaves such youthful things behind him, his guitar will be quite proper as he has now become a folk singing intellectual. When he comes home after a busy day at work, his guitar is his finest outlet from business pressures as it will give him the maximum dividend of relaxation from a minimum of investment of time, study, and effort. And when he finally hangs up his town suit for his robe of retirement, his trusty old guitar will be the pride of his home – his pal on the porch – his friend while fishing, and his hobby while hunting.

"*So there you have it.* From East to West, from rags to riches, rompers to retirement. *Mr. Guitar,* whose use and ubiquity makes the instrument for every person, every place, and every purpose.

"I know you think there must be an end to it somewhere, but I can truthfully tell you there is no end, because old guitarists never die, they just fake away!"

***"I first started writing for the guitar because of my love for the instrument. It really pleases me to see the dedication of today's young musicians. We get loads of correspondence from young musicians, and I can tell by their questions that music is more than just a passing interest."***

**– Mel Bay**

# VIGNETTES

On the following pages are just a few of many vignettes, or short sketches, from Mel Bay's life which he has related to many people, including this author, through the years. They give you some insight into the uniqueness of Mel Bay and his experiences. Just imagine having him tell them to you in person – a twinkle in his eyes, grin on his face, and always capped with a hearty laugh.

*"We had to wear this hot wool uniform when we played at ball games," says Mel Bay about one of his "gigs" in the 1940s. "In hot weather we would have to go out into the scalding sun and play. That uniform was like wearing a wet wool blanket. In vengeance, when the umpires would come onto the field we would play 'Three Blind Mice,' which always got a loud cheer from the crowd."*

## *Not born in a log cabin, but close!*

In speaking of his beginnings, Mel Bay jokingly says that he was not born in a manger in a stable, or in a log cabin. But he was born in a humble frame house in the little sawmill town of Bunker, in the Ozark hills of Missouri. And he was born ahead of his time, literally – prematurely at only 2 $^{1}/_{2}$ pounds.

That is a precarious beginning today. It was much more precarious back then. There were no incubators or modern feeding systems as we have today. Mel's mother would put him in the warming oven of the wood-burning cook stove to keep him warm while she worked around the house.

Whether that tiny start affected his size today would not be provable. Mr. Bay's general physique could have always been described as slight and refined, rather than huge and heavy-boned.

Of himself, Mel has this to say: "My hands are on the small side – to the point where I had to stretch pretty hard to play a full-sized guitar. "So when I got far enough along in the music world that I could afford it, I went to John D'Angelico, the well-known guitar maker in New York, and asked him to make me a tailor-made model.

*Mel's friend Al Valenti as a top New York guitarist...circa 1935. The autograph reads: "To Melbourne Bay, Wishing you the best of luck with your new guitar."*

"I asked for a thinner, more refined neck, and a cutaway in the body so that I would have more movement down the neck."

That was the start of a model that became so popular that D'Angelico named it *The Mel Bay Guitar.*

Today, the value of a vintage, handmade D'Angelico *Mel Bay Guitar* can reach the $100,000 range.

***Guitar Player magazine says about Mel Bay:***

***"He is the George Washington of guitar instruction."***

## *Mel Bay's plot to get some sleep*

Young Mel Bay was working night and day in St. Louis – teaching banjo and guitar, playing in groups, and scratching out a living. Whenever he could break away from this tiring schedule, he would slip back to his home in DeSoto. There his mother would wash his clothes, fix him some good meals, and he could catch up on sleep.

There was *one problem.*

Mel would have to sleep in an upstairs bedroom with his brother, who was an avid hunter. His brother's favorite Sunday morning schedule was to set the alarm clock for 5:45, get up, get dressed, gather up his hunting gear, and set off for the woods and fields.

One Saturday night Mel came dragging in after long hard hours of playing with a group for a dance. As he slipped into the bedroom where his brother was sleeping, he saw that the alarm clock was set for 5:45, and he could guess what would happen. He would just be getting some good sleep, and his brother would jump up and start his usual commotion. Mel couldn't stand the thought of going through that ordeal.

Just before 3:30 a.m. he set the clock ahead to ring in just a few minutes, so his brother would get out of the room and he could get some sleep! Mel slipped into bed, and at 3:30 a.m., the alarm jumped into its loud, metallic ringing.

His brother charged out of bed and went through his ritual of getting dressed, gathering up his hunting gear, and stomping out the door.

Mel heard his brother start the car and drive away.

Finally he could get some sleep!

His brother, once out in the woods where he planned to hunt squirrels, couldn't figure out why it stayed dark so long. He watched for daylight. Finally, after much waiting, he looked across a field and saw a farm house with a light on. He walked over and knocked on the door.

The farmer gingerly opened the door. Then, recognizing Mel's brother, asked: "What are you doing at this hour?"

"Hunting squirrels!" Mel's brother announced.

The farmer scratched his head, then with a smirk, said: "Ain't 4:30 in the morning a mite early?"

Mel laughs when he tells that story today.

He says his brother took a dim view of the incident.

***By 1933 (he was then 20 years old), Mel Bay was performing regularly on radio stations in St. Louis, and soon became the most sought-after guitarist in the area.***

***When a recording studio or a big band needed a guitarist, Mel Bay was brought in.***

***"I became what's known as a professional musician's musician," Mel says.***

## *Why do people buy so much yeast?*

"During the Prohibition years of 1920 to 1932, when the making and sale of alcoholic beverages was forbidden by federal law, a lot of people secretly made their own home brew," says Mel Bay.

"They would put it into glass bottles and cap it with metal caps and let it sit until it was ready to drink.

"I was working in my dad's grocery store in DeSoto, Missouri, and a lot of people would come in to buy a can of malt, a cake of yeast, and sugar. Our preacher must have suspected what was going on, and one day when he was in our store he watched, then came up and asked me why so many people bought malt – and yeast.

"'To make bread to eat,' I quickly replied, as my dad always said. He looked at me with a mischievous glint in his eyes, smiled, and asked: 'Don't those bottle caps hurt their teeth?'"

## *Learning how to sell: "Is your mother here?"*

After making a speech to the National Association of Music Merchants where he was on the Board of Directors, Mel was asked the question: "Did you take training in business and salesmanship, or how did you learn to sell?"

Mel explained that he pretty much picked it up on his own, beginning at an early age when he had to sell something in order to eat.

"When I was 10 years old I sold copies of *Grit,* a general interest newspaper-like magazine published back East," Mel related. "I learned how to be the top salesman by the approach I made at each door."

"And what was that?" asked the man in the audience.

"Well, when a woman answered the door, regardless of her age, I would always ask: "Is your mother here?"

## *A snowstorm of music covers the railroad tracks*

When Mel Bay was a student in high school (1927-31) in DeSoto, Missouri, he played cymbals in the booster band. It was announced that the president of the Missouri Pacific Railroad would be coming to DeSoto by train, and the booster band was readied to give Mr. L. W. Baldwin a rousing welcome.

The big day came.

Mel and his group waited anxiously by the railroad station.

Finally, they heard the train coming, and with a stack of sheet music on a stand in front of each band member, they struck up a lively piece. They kept glancing up from their music to watch for the train – and here it came!

Mel says: "The smoke was flowing straight back from the big engine, down over the top of the line of cars, which meant that the engineer was really pouring the coal to it!"

The band kept blasting out its rousing welcome music, and Mel kept clapping his cymbals with full vigor and enthusiasm.

When would the train slow down and stop?

It didn't!

It thundered right past the band, the crowd of people, and the railroad station. And as it did, giant gusts of air picked up all of the sheets of music and swirled them high into the sky. As the caboose at the end of the train sped past, and the air calmed down, sheets of music began to flutter and settle down like a snowstorm, all over the tracks.

Then all was quiet.

The train was gone, the band was silent. The crowd that had assembled with such anticipation stood somber and puzzled.

What went wrong?

The explanation: Somebody had forgotten to tell Mr. Baldwin to advise the train crew that he wanted to make a stop in DeSoto!

## *"Boy, you are the best car salesman in the world!"*

As a teenager in DeSoto, Missouri, where his dad operated Bay's Market, Mel's vehicle for transportation was an old, beat-up car with the brand name of Essex.

"A real piece of junk," says Mel, with many unfond memories of the problems he had just keeping it running.

"I had paid $25 for it – a fair amount of money back in those days," he says.

While looking around in St. Louis, where he was playing whatever jobs he could find, and teaching at the Hugo School of Music, Mel spotted a canary-yellow 1932 Ford Cabriolet, with a rumble seat in back, on a dealer's lot.

What a beauty!

It was priced at $250.

Already learning how to barter, Mel offered the salesman $200 in cash, plus his old Essex.

The salesman asked: "Where is your car?"

"Down in DeSoto," Mel replied.

"Do you live in DeSoto?" the salesman asked.

"Yes," replied Mel.

The salesman knew about the poor roads and hills between St. Louis and DeSoto, so he asked: "Can you drive your car up here?"

"Sure," replied Mel with confidence.

The salesman then said: "If you can drive that car all the way into this dealership, you've got a deal!"

The problem was that Mel's car was not running at all. The engine just would no longer work (because of a busted piston). So, Mel had his dad and brother tow the old junker up and down the hills until they got to St. Louis. They stopped on a hill above the dealership. Then they gave his car a big shove and Mel coasted it into the dealer's lot and parked it.

Mel paid the dealer the $200, got into his new yellow Ford, and happily drove away.

Part of the deal was that Mel would bring the Ford back after a month of owning it and have the mechanic check it over to see if everything was okay. So Mel drove back to the dealership and the mechanic came out to get the car and check it over.

The mechanic immediately recognized that bright yellow car, turned to Mel and told him that the boss wanted to talk to him. Somewhat reluctantly, Mel walked into the dealer's office.

The dealer pulled out the key to Mel's old Essex, laid it on the desk, looked at Mel and asked: "Boy, can you show my service manager how to start that damn car you brought in here?"

Mel had to admit that this was one reason he had traded it in – he couldn't get it started.

The owner looked hard at Mel, then asked: "Young man, what do you do for a living?"

Mel told him that he was struggling along at a number of jobs – teaching at the Hugo School of Music, playing on KMOX, working dance jobs.

The dealer looked hard at him again and asked: "How would you like to come work for me?"

Completely surprised and puzzled, Mel finally managed to ask: "What would I do?" The dealer firmly replied: "You would sell cars!"

"Sell cars?" Mel asked with continued puzzlement, .... "but I am a musician!"

"Well," said the dealer, "anybody who can make a trade like you did has to be the best used car salesman in the world!"

Looking back at that unusual experience, Mel says today: "I decided to stick with music, and I have never been sorry that I did."

## *A slap in the face: Mel Bay strikes back!*

Mel Bay's 1924 Essex coupe with a rumble seat was very noticeable and popular around DeSoto High School when he was wheeling around in it. The homecoming committee asked Mel if he would drive it in the big parade, with the Queen of Homecoming riding in the open rumble seat where she could wave to the rows of onlookers on both sides of the street.

Mel Bay kindly obliged, and drove his car, carrying the queen, in the big parade, for two years in a row. He was basking in the glory of it all, but fate dealt him a bitter blow. The homecoming committee informed him that they would no longer need his services – in his old Essex car. "One of your classmates has just bought a new Ford V-8, and we will use that in this year's parade."

That was like a slap in the face!

Beaten down, Mel Bay was in a slump because his car was too antiquated to be in the parade. But as he sat and commiserated with himself, a brilliant thought came to mind. He remembered how a skywriting plane had flown over DeSoto and, spewing out a big stream of smoke, had written the words "Coca Cola." Mel had a friend who was a mechanic, and he asked his friend how the pilot could make the plane spew out the smoke.

The mechanic had the simple answer: "He just pours some castor oil into the gas tank."

Mel's first move was to purchase a pint of castor oil – no problem. Next, during the big bonfire celebration the night before the big parade, Mel simply crept over to the unattended new Ford V-8 and poured the castor oil into the gas tank.

The next morning was bright and sunny, and people crowded both sides of the street watching the various marchers and floats pass by. They looked for the car bearing the beautiful homecoming queen.

What they saw was a huge cloud of billowing smoke – which, as Mel today laughingly says: "Got so bad that you couldn't see the queen or the coach riding with her – they had to stop the parade!" They then put the football captain and the queen on the local fire truck.

Did young Mel Bay have a devilish streak in him? "No, just youthful ingenuity," Mel says – with a devilish smile.

## *The scar on the finger: A reminder of the Depression*

Young Mel Bay, like millions of others across the United States in the early 1930s, was doing whatever he could to scratch out a living – something to earn enough money just to live on. Mel was teaching music to other young people who were also suffering from the wretched economy – they were having problems paying him.

"I played in the joints around town for tips so I could eat," Mel recalls.

"One morning I had a donut and a cup of coffee for breakfast – that took the two nickels I had in my pocket, so then I was broke. I went all day, teaching, without anything to eat. After teaching, I went around to the joints and played until I had two nickels and eight pennies in my pocket from tips. I went into a little delicatessen on Union Avenue in St. Louis and bought a little can of vienna sausages, some crackers, and some milk. I was so hungry that in my haste to open the can of sausages I broke the little metal key, then in tearing the can open I severely cut my second finger."

Not having money to go to a doctor, Mel simply held his thumb over the cut while he wolfed down the sausages, crackers, and milk. And then, since this was before Band-Aids®, Mel says that he held his thumb over the cut for almost three days until it began to heal.

Today he holds up that finger and you can still see the scar – just one of many reminders of those Depression days.

"But, we lived through it – we survived – and I think we are better for having lived through some tough times," Mel says philosophically.

"That's when we learned that the biggest part of good luck is hard work!"

## *Other guitarists who overcame injuries*

This is not to "top" Mel Bay's story of how he injured his finger, and overcame the injury to keep on playing – but simply to add a couple of other testimonials. In 1963, Johnny Smith, who by then was well known as one of the top – if not the top – jazz guitarists, was flying his own plane to engagements around the United States. He was in his plane, probably in a hurry, and somehow got the third finger of his left hand caught in the track under the seat as he moved it forward. In an agonizing second he had torn half an inch off the end of this finger!

Fortunately he was able to get to a good surgeon, Dr. Jack King, who performed a near miracle. The surgeon grafted Smith's finger to the palm of his hand so that new tissues could grow on, then at the proper time surgically removed the finger with its new tissue at the end.

It took many months to train the new finger to the strings and frets, but Johnny Smith persevered, and went on playing for many years.

## *Django Reinhardt*

Django Reinhardt, who was to become a world-renowned guitarist, was born in 1910 in Belgium into a gypsy family, the son of an entertainer who worked in a traveling show. Young Reinhardt, while traveling Europe with this show, learned guitar, banjo, and violin. As a young man he worked as a street musician in the Montmarte area of Paris. He married, and his wife made candles as the caravan moved around Europe.

One night in 1928 (when Django was 18) the caravan was camped on the outskirts of Paris. When some candles caught fire, Reinhardt and his wife were terribly burned. After hospital treatment, Reinhardt was left with two withered fingers on his left hand.

For most guitarists it might have been the end of a career, but Reinhardt persevered and developed his own unique technique using the first two fingers of his left hand, with the withered third and fourth fingers helping out only on some simple chords. The brilliant solos that he played, often at the most astonishing speed, were played entirely with the first two fingers of his injured hand.

Source: *The Jazz Guitarist* by Maurice J. Summerfield

## *Nobody knows you? Have yourself paged!*

When Mel Bay first joined the American Federation of Musicians Union in St. Louis in the 1930s, he was an unknown.

"I used to go into the big union hall and just stand around. I didn't know anybody and they didn't know me, and I was too shy to bounce around like a politician and introduce myself," Mel recalls.

"One time when I was standing alone I heard the sergeant at arms of the union come in and yell: 'Telephone call for Mr. Herb Rathert of KMOX!'

"Mr. Rathert walked out to answer the call.

"That gave me an idea," Mel says, "so I began having myself paged: 'Mr. Mel Bay! Telephone call for Mr. Mel Bay!' the sergeant at arms would yell out above the din of the union members talking to each other.

"I was talking to Frank Sedlach, a saxophone player, when the sergeant at arms came up and tapped me on the shoulder and asked: 'Do you have an office down here?'

"I hesitated, then said: 'No, I don't – why do you ask?'

"'Well,' he replied: 'You get more phone calls in here than anybody else!'"

Mel smiles and says: "That was when I learned that it pays to advertise!"

***"I've put more time in this business than anyone I've ever known and I never considered it work. It's a way of life for me and I have no intentions of retiring. If I did, I'd die."***

**– Mel Bay**

# *How Mel met May*

When Mel Bay first started teaching guitar in St. Louis in 1934, one of his pupils was a girl from Webster Groves (one of St. Louis' oldest suburbs) named May Gebelein. Mel had reservations about asking a student for a date, but after a few weeks, he worked up the courage to do so.

In an effort to impress her, Mel took her for a long drive south into his native Ozark mountains for a picnic at Lake Killarney.

On the way back, he hit a cow (there was an open range policy then which allowed cattle to wander across the roads). Hitting the big animal wrecked the car and the 'newsome twosome' came home in a tow truck.

With his impish grin, always evident when telling a tale, Mel says: "A local paper published a story with the headline 'Mel Bay Kills Cow While Shooting the Bull.'"

*Mel and May Bay attending a music convention circa 1960.*

# *A shortcut through a cornfield*

Back in 1937, Mel Bay had a little band that played jobs out in small towns, and one night they had a job in Goldman, Missouri, a tiny town about 35 miles south of St. Louis.

The band was composed of six musicians who would team up in three cars and meet at the job site.

One particular night it was agreed that they would meet at "the Walgreen Drug Store."

Mel and his partner waited at the Walgreen store. They waited and they waited.

Finally they got on the phone and started calling around and discovered that the other two cars were at another Walgreen store in a different location.

Time was getting short, so the other two drivers agreed to come to meet Mel, and then he could lead them to the job.

Eventually there were three cars racing over the winding country roads, with Mel in the lead.

Abruptly he came to a sharp right turn that he couldn't manage, so he plowed right straight ahead into a cornfield.

The other two cars, racing too fast to make the turn, followed him right into the thick of the corn.

After they had all squished to a stop in the heavy stalks and soft earth, everybody got out of the cars.

Suddenly five guys were glaring at Mel and asking: "What-in-hell are we doing in this cornfield?"

Mel's quick reply: "This is a shortcut!"

## *A piano player stings a singer*

"One night our band was backing up a girl singer. She wasn't very good, and she was blaming others for her problems," Mel Bay relates.

"After singing a number very poorly she saw the reaction of the audience, then in frustration turned to the pianist and said: 'I just don't like the way you are accompanying me!'"

The pianist beckoned her to lean toward him, then cupping his hand whispered into her ear: "Madam, I play on the white keys, and I play on the black keys. But Madam, you are singing in the cracks!"

## *A bad comedian blames the band*

"One time we were playing backup for a comedian," Mel Bay recalls.

"His jokes were falling flat.

"The harder he tried, the worse the reaction from the audience.

"Full of frustration and anger, he looked over to the leader of the band and fumed: 'Look at your band! They are all sitting there half asleep!'

"The leader replied: 'Well, you put 'em there!'"

## *Wrong turn, wrong river – wrong town!*

On a bitterly cold winter night (25 degrees below zero) in 1947, Mel and the band played at an Elks Club banquet in Hannibal, Missouri – the town made famous by Mark Twain. The city of Hannibal is situated on the Mississippi River about halfway between St. Louis and the Iowa border, to the north. The event ended about midnight, so Mel and his tired partners climbed into a very cold automobile and started the long drive back to St. Charles, Missouri, across the Missouri River, west of St. Louis.

At least, so they thought.

Mel was asleep in the front seat of the car when the driver said that he had crossed the river, so they must be in St. Charles.

Mel sat up and looked around.

They had crossed the river, all right, but it was the Mississippi River up at Keokuk, Iowa!

They had headed north instead of south.

So back they went, until Mel finally asked the driver to stop so that he could get a cup of coffee.

Then he pointed out the window to a building and said: "You see that building over there – that's where we were playing that job just four hours ago!"

They were back in Hannibal.

Now they could head south until they crossed the Missouri River and finally arrive at their destination at St. Charles – as the sun was coming up.

"Such is the exciting life of musicians!" Mel says.

***During his heavy traveling days, Mel Bay was driving through Indiana and stopped at a service station to get gas. He handed the young lad at the station his credit card.***

***"Mel Bay?" the boy asked, wide-eyed. "Are you the one who writes down the chords? Man, you got my hands hurtin' all the time!"***

## *A "bug-gy" compliment for Mel Bay Books*

Among the many and varied compliments that Mel Bay has gotten from guitar players who have used his books, an unusual one came to him not from a guitar player, but from a dealer.

"I like your books, Mel," said the dealer.

"That's nice," said Mel, wondering what was coming next. "Why do you like them?"

Said the dealer: "Because you don't use any glue to bind them!"

Puzzled, Mel asked: "Why do you like that?"

Replied the man: "Because other books draw cockroaches – they like to eat the glue. Mel Bay books – no glue – no cockroaches!"

*In Tulsa, Oklahoma, Mel Bay presents a plaque to the people in the store that sold the largest number of his method books that year.*

## *A brief encounter – "Who was that man?"*

"I was having dinner with a music magazine editor in a restaurant on 5th Avenue in New York," Mel relates as his mind bounces back over the years.

"I glanced up and noticed a couple walking our way. The dress of the woman was an obvious sign that she was what we then called 'a lady of the evening...'

"As the couple walked past us, the man suddenly stopped, turned to me and said: 'Are you Mel Bay?'

"I said: 'Yes, I am, but I must confess that I don't recognize you.'

"The man replied curtly: 'Just forget that you ever saw me!' and hurriedly walked away."

Says Mel Bay with a hearty laugh: "To this day, I have no idea who that man was!"

*During the 1950s and '60s when Mel Bay was commuting to New York City to write arrangements for the big music publishers, he often stopped to look at the big city and think back to his humble beginnings in the hills of Missouri.*

## *"Man on the moon before guitar is taught in schools"*

Back in 1954 Mel Bay was invited to talk to music teachers attending the National Association of Music Educators in Washington, D.C. He considered this a rare opportunity in his continuous crusade to sell the merits of the guitar as an important musical instrument.

First, he demonstrated how his chord system made it easier and simpler to play the guitar, and how the versatility of the instrument enabled it to fit into many music situations. Then Mel boldly predicted that some day the guitar would be taught in nearly all schools – public, private, and parochial.

After he had made that prediction, a man in the audience stood up and said: "Mr. Bay, I enjoyed your program and found it interesting. However, I believe that before you see the guitar taught in our schools, you will see a man walk on the moon, and you will see Mississippi go Republican!"

Today, Mel Bay laughs and says: "Now I've seen all of these things happen!"

*A guitar class at Webster Groves, Missouri, High School in the 1960s. Behind the students: Dave Mortland, guitar teacher; Hans Lemcke, head of the music department, and Mel Bay, who was "coaching" this particular session.*

## *The strange case of the man who couldn't say "Mel Bay!"*

After he had become well known as a musician, teacher, writer, and publisher, Mel Bay began to get invitations to serve on boards of national music associations, to speak at conventions, and to judge music contests. He was invited to Hamilton, Ontario, Canada, to judge the string division of a big contest.

Dressed for the occasion in their tuxedos, Mel and other adjudicators were sitting up on a big stage awaiting formal introductions to the audience at the final awards program.

The Master of Ceremonies who was making the introductions seemed to be having great difficulty with names, and several times turned to ask Mel Bay: "What is your name?"

Mel, getting somewhat aggravated at this, and noticing that the Emcee might have been sipping something other than coffee, tried to get him on the right track. He thought he was being helpful when he said: "My name is *BAY* – like Hudson *Bay*, or Chesapeake *Bay!*"

Mel thought that this simple association should certainly be of help to the man.

But, when the big moment came, and the Emcee stepped up to make the next announcement, he said: "Ladies and gentlemen! It gives me great pleasure to introduce a very well-known musician and publisher who is the official judge of the string division – *Mr. Chester Hudson!*"

## *"Not you – I mean Mel Bay – the guy who writes the books!"*

"One night – in the 1970s when our Kirkwood store was doing well – we had about a five or six-inch snow, and it was still snowing when I got up in the morning," Mel Bay relates.

"It was about 8:30 when I got to the store. The sidewalk in front was ankle deep, so I decided to go out and shovel it clean," he continues.

"I was making good progress, when about 9 o'clock, along came a very distinguished gentleman.

"He walked up to the front door of the store, then stopped and turned, looked at me and asked: 'Do you work here?'

"Yes, I work here," Mel answered.

Then the man asked: "Does Mr. Mel Bay ever come here?"

Mel answered, with a quirky smile: "Yes, he comes in sometimes."

Then the gentleman asked: "I wonder if it would be possible for me to see Mr. Mel Bay?"

Mel replied: "Well, sir, you are talking to him."

The man shook his head disgustedly and said: "No, I don't mean you – I mean Mel Bay, the man who writes the books!"

"Sir, I am that man," Mel replied.

"Shoveling sidewalks?" the man asked with a puzzled look.

"Yes, somebody has to do it," Mel replied. Then he said: "Let's go inside."

It turned out that the man was Dean of Music at a well-known university.

Later he wrote an article about his encounter.

He penned: "Guess who I met while he was out shoveling snow – Mel Bay!"

## *Johnny Smith plays a practical joke on Mel*

As you talk to professional musicians you learn that swapping funny stories and playing practical jokes on each other helped lift them out of some of the drudgery of the business.

Johnny Smith likes to tell about the fishing trick he pulled on Mel Bay in Colorado. Johnny was teaching Mel the sophisticated techniques of "long-line fishing" on a lake.

Johnny tells it this way: "Mel got into his boat, and drove across the lake. He had picked up his rod and reel and let out a lot of line over the side for trolling. Then he stretched out across the boat. He had his big Stetson hat on his head, a cigar in his mouth, and had his fishing rod across his lap. He was really relaxed!

"I came along several hundred yards behind and slowly followed Mel's boat. I looked over the side and saw Mel's line and bait drifting alongside my boat... So, I simply reached down, picked up Mel's line, and gave it a real healthy tug.

"Mel lurched up out of his reclining position, dropped the cigar out of his mouth, lost his big hat over the side, grabbed his pole and jerked until the line was tight, then yelled: 'Man, I have got a big one!'"

Johnny Smith related this story at the Sheldon Music Hall in St. Louis, Missouri on the evening of Friday, October 25, 1996, when Mel was presented with the Lifetime Achievement Award by the Guitar Foundation of America.

*Three of the string music world's "greats" – Mel Bay, Johnny Smith and jazz tenor banjoist John Becker – get together in Colorado to do some fishing, some reminiscing, and to swap jokes.*

## *An objective look by someone who is not a part of the music world...*

"As I look at the life of Mel Bay, I recognize a very unique man.

"I see that he has musical talent. But I also see that he has many other attributes which have contributed to his success: Hard work, perseverance, dedication, loyalty, courtesy – an endless list of attributes that you might find in a Boy Scout manual.

"He never pretended to be pure, or an angel. In fact, he often pokes fun at himself about what a rascal he was at times.

"Yet, the good in the man is what I see, and to me, that wipes out any faults or misdeeds someone else might attach to him.

"To me, he is one of the greatest guys I have ever met!"

– an anonymous member of the
Kirkwood Coffee Club

# *Confrontation at Cripple Creek*

During one of their visits to their retreat in Colorado, Mel and May decided to show some guests from Florida the old gold mining town of Cripple Creek, south of their retreat and about 50 miles west of Colorado Springs. To fit the setting, all were dressed in appropriate western garb.

"I was wearing my big Stetson, western shirt and jeans, and of course, boots," says Mel.

"We eventually went to one of those outdoor, Chuck Wagon beans-and-burgers and western-music places," Mel relates.

"We sat at a table enjoying the simple food, the fresh air, and the music. The young band leader recognized me, and asked me if I would favor them by coming up and playing the guitar," Mel says.

"I reluctantly agreed, walked up, and was handed a nice Stratocaster guitar," Mel further relates.

"Before I could start to play anything a big man in the audience yelled out: 'Do you know how play "San Antonio Rose"?'"

Before he could answer yes, Mel's quick-quip mind ("I don't always know what I am going to pop out with") spouted: "Oh, so we have somebody here from Texas! You know, if there had been a back door in the Alamo we wouldn't even have that state!"

There was a loud response of laughing and applause from the audience.

Then Mel played his own arrangement of "San Antonio Rose."

After acknowledging the applause for this special performance, Mel nodded and thanked the audience, then returned to his table. He was busy talking to his guests when he felt a tap on his shoulder. Mel turned, looked up, and saw the big man from Texas towering over him. Mel cringed as he thought back to his quick quip about the Alamo. He expected a real lashing of some kind.

But he was pleasantly surprised when the big man gave him a faint smile, then said: "Say – you're pretty good!"

After overcoming his surprise, Mel was able to come up with: "Thank you."

Then the big man asked: "Ain't you a professional?"

Mel (wanting to be modest and also to maintain his anonymity) replied: "No, I am not a professional – do I look like a musician?"

The man replied: “No, but you sure sound like one.”

Mel came back with: “Well, I wish I were a professional – that would be something!”

The man came back with: “Well, you are now!” And with that he stuffed something into Mel’s shirt pocket and walked away.

After a suitable time to allow the man to return to his table, Mel cautiously reached into his shirt pocket and gingerly pulled out what the big man had stuffed into it.

Mel’s guests from Florida and Mrs. Bay broke out with big western guffaws.

When Mel unfolded a piece of paper, he saw that it was a one-dollar bill.

## *Chet Atkins' humor*

Anybody who knows Mel Bay will quickly attest to the fact that he has a good sense of humor – and that he has his own sense of humor. But he also appreciates the humor of many of his old buddies, like Chet Atkins.

Here's a little story that Mel tells about Chet's sense of humor:

"In his early days of learning how to play the guitar, it seemed that Chet Atkins was always strumming the same chord.

"Finally his dad said to him: 'For God's sake why don't you play like the other guys do – they play all over the guitar, but you just sit there and play that same chord!'

"Chet stopped strumming and explained: 'They're still looking around for this chord – I've found it!'"

## *The wit of Chet Atkins*

Mel Bay cites another example:

"One Sunday morning I picked up Chet, Boots Randolf and Floyd Cramer, and took them to the airport. They were going to Springfield, Missouri.

"My father and brother Bill were sitting at the boarding area for the Springfield trip. I introduced Dad to Chet.

"Dad said: 'I'm sorry, but I didn't recognize you wearing those dark glasses.'

"Chet quipped: 'When I'm with Mel I don't want to be recognized.'"

## *Does every musician know Mel Bay?*

In a poor, rundown neighborhood of North St. Louis, Missouri, there is a unique African-American man by the name of Otis Woodard. Born in Birmingham, Alabama, he spent time in the U.S. Marine Corps and today he lives by his strong Christian belief that God put him here to help others.

Otis operates the Lutheran Outreach Center – a gathering place for food and clothes and materials for those who need them. He wears outlandish costumes – long flowing robes and beads so that everybody who sees him, including the police, can immediately know: "That's Otis!"

This author took a pickup load of old storm windows down for Otis to give to people whom, he says: "Don't even have windows!"

As we unloaded the windows and chatted about Otis' work, I recalled that he had visited our church in Kirkwood, had played the ukulele and sang to us about his work.

So I asked the usual question: "Otis, do you know Mel Bay?" Otis gave me a big smile and said: "Sure – I have a ukulele book signed by him!"

Just one more example.

Wherever you may go – anywhere in the world – you will meet someone who has met Mel Bay – or used his books – or both!

*Otis Woodard, a native of Birmingham, Alabama, now lives in a poor area of north St. Louis where he operates the Lutheran Outreach, a place that supplies food, clothing, building materials, and other helpful items to the needy people in the area. Otis is a man of many talents, and is proud of a ukulele book signed many years ago by Mel Bay.*

## *How the world looked from the bandstand*

When I first asked Mel Bay to tell me about some of his experiences up on the bandstand looking out at a variety of people in a vast variety of places, I asked: "Mel, how did the world look to you from up there?"

In a Mel Bay quippy way he replied: "There was so much smoke I couldn't see the world!"

He wasn't completely kidding about that, he said in a more serious tone.

“So many of the joints we played in were noisy and smoky, and the people seemed to be so busy smoking, drinking, and talking, that they didn't know, or didn't care where the music was coming from.

“That's what I think of when I tell you that there is little glamour in this business,” Mel adds with a thoughtful look on his face.

*Mel Bay (front row, center) had the chance to view the bandstand from a different angle during a concert to honor him at the Guitar Foundation of America's International Convention in St. Louis October 25, 1996.*

## *Sometimes, someone asks: "Who is Mel Bay?"*

To be objective in this book, it must be noted that *not everyone* we meet knows who Mel Bay is. I was talking with a young man and his wife; he is a writer, so I mentioned that I was writing *The Mel Bay Story*.

He gave me a blank look and asked: "Who is Mel Bay?"

Before I could explain, or be chagrined at his question, his wife quickly chipped in: "I play guitar – I've used his books!"

And that's the way it goes. In the world of those who don't play an instrument, and never shop in music stores, Mel Bay may be an unknown. But in the huge world of millions who know and use his books, he is a legend.

Some people ask Mel Bay how he learned to play the guitar. He frequently quips: "I did it just like everybody else – I bought a guitar and learned from a Mel Bay book!"

## *A musician's life – enter through the kitchen!*

"It's been a good life," Mel Bay always says when talking about his long career as a musician, teacher, and music publishing businessman. But as you talk to him and pick around at some of the details, you realize that it wasn't all glow and glamour.

You learn that much of his life was long hours of hard work – on the road, on the bandstand, in his office – wherever.

He tells the joke about a Jehovah's Witness asking him if he wants to go to heaven, and his answer was: "If I get there, I'll have to *go in through the kitchen* with all the other musicians."

## *Mel Bay on the retail music business*

"Music retailing is a business you have to love to succeed in. There are lots of frustrations, long hours, and other problems.

"Every member of the Bay family has spent hours behind the counter of our St. Louis retail store.

"I think that one of the reasons we have been blessed with success in publishing is that we have always loved the retail side of the music business and we have felt especially sensitive to the needs of the retailer.

"Our publishing company is run in a similar fashion to our retail store.

"On any given day you will find us doing whatever is needed to keep things rolling.

"No matter how busy we become, I hope we never lose the feeling of a close knit, hard working family business."

(Author's note: This was written in 1978 – the basic thinking is still evident today.)

***"We aren't in competition with anyone here at Mel Bay Publications. We are creators, not followers. When I am asked how I feel about others writing their own versions of my method books, I always explain how it is too little, too late. I concentrate on doing my own job...not on who is copying me!"***

**– Mel Bay**

## *Can you write for Mel Bay Publishing Company?*

Hundreds of aspiring new music writers contact Mel and William Bay every year to ask if they can write for them.

When we asked William how he selects writers he gave this answer: "Basically, we have several ways to evaluate a new book. Our staff may feel that a particular book would be necessary, and we will contact one of our writers (they have a list of more than 600) and ask him or her to write a book based on that general concept.

"We do have a large number of 'name' performing musicians who contact us and state that they would like to write manuscripts. In some cases, this works out beautifully. In some cases, it does not.

"Writing a book takes a lot of work and it helps to have a feel for what students relate to. Being a good performer does not automatically mean that you are a good writer.

"I am sure we are no different than many other publishers in that some of our finest books were written by people who spend most of their time teaching."

***"We are all musicians here, and we stress products that are musically correct and that fill a need. We try to avoid gimmicks."***

**– Mel Bay**

## *How does Mel Bay handle "the generation gap"?*

Mel Bay thinks that constant talk about the "generation gap" is really "an old song" that he has heard for many years.

"For example," he says, "let's jump all the way back to 1928 when I was young and playing a popular song called 'Doodle De Do.'"

"My dad – then being the 'older generation' to me, stopped me one day and asked: 'What is that thing you're playing?'

"I answered: 'It's a new song called "Doodle De Do."'

"My dad looked aghast and asked: 'Doodle De what?' I answered: 'Doodle De Do.'

"Then my dad made a statement that I have heard many times through the years – and probably have made it myself at times. He said, with firm emphasis: 'No wonder you kids are all going bad!'"

Then Mel adds: "His kind of song at that time was called 'Golden Slippers,' mostly because that's what he grew up with – just as every generation grows up with its own music, which sounds crazy to the older generation – at any time in history."

Thinking ahead to what's in store for the next generation, Mel Bay advises youngsters who are interested in music to go into it for the enjoyment of it.

During the course of a day in his Kirkwood music store Mel and his staff talk to people from as young as four and five years old to some in their 90s – that covers many years, several generations, and many types of music and preferences.

Mel and his staff are courteous to all ages.

Mel doesn't advise any youngster to plunge into music with the thought of becoming a professional performer.

He didn't start that way – he gradually worked his way into it. And he feels that any person who has the talent and drive for a professional career will gradually discover that.

He says: "If they definitely feel that they want to become a music teacher or play with a symphony, they can pursue that dream. But if they just want music for fun – if it gives them self-satisfaction – then I think that is a worthwhile pursuit. It adds another dimension to your life!"

PEARSON MUSIC COMPANY

is proud to present

an appearance by world-renown

Guitarist and Author

**MEL BAY**

Sat., Nov. 14, at 2:00 PM at Silas Creek location

Mel Bay will autograph copies of his

method book which has sold over

7 MILLION copies worldwide.

Accompanying Mel Bay will be Guitarist

**Richard Matteson**

who teaches at Pearson Music Co.

Richard will autograph copies of his new books,

"Folksongs from the Appalachians"

and "Early Hymns of America"

for solo guitar.

Don't miss this opportunity to meet guitar

legend Mel Bay and get an autographed book.

This will probably be Mel Bay's

last visit to the Triad.

*This advertisement announced a special event in Winston-Salem, North Carolina, in the early 1990s when Mel was nearly 80 years old. Mel laughs at the last two lines with a chuckle, and says: "So that's what they think about me at this age!"*

# Awards and Accolades

Through the years Mel Bay has received many awards, plaques, and proclamations for his contributions to the world of music, and the world in general. We will not burden you, the reader, by showing all of these. Instead, we will show you a select sampling to give you an idea of what others think of this man...

*The Kirkwood Chamber of Commerce presented the award at left to Mel Bay, "a living legend in the world of music...and an unparalleled success in the world of business," on November 12, 1996.*

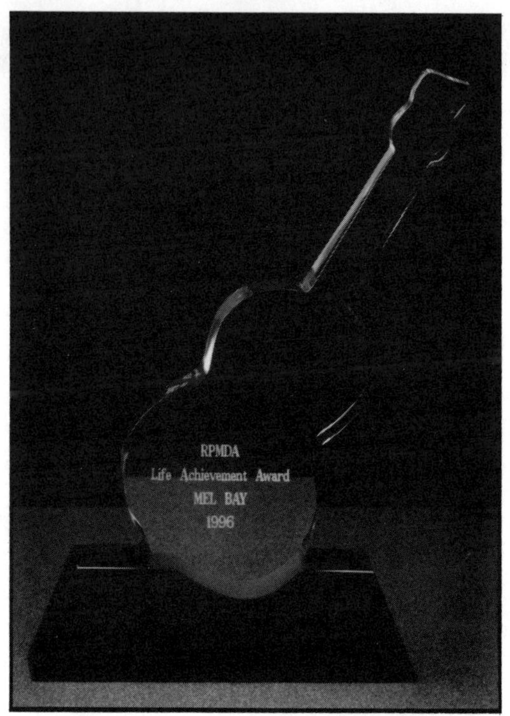


*Lifetime Achievement Award presented to Mel Bay in 1996 by the Retail Print Music Dealers Association.*

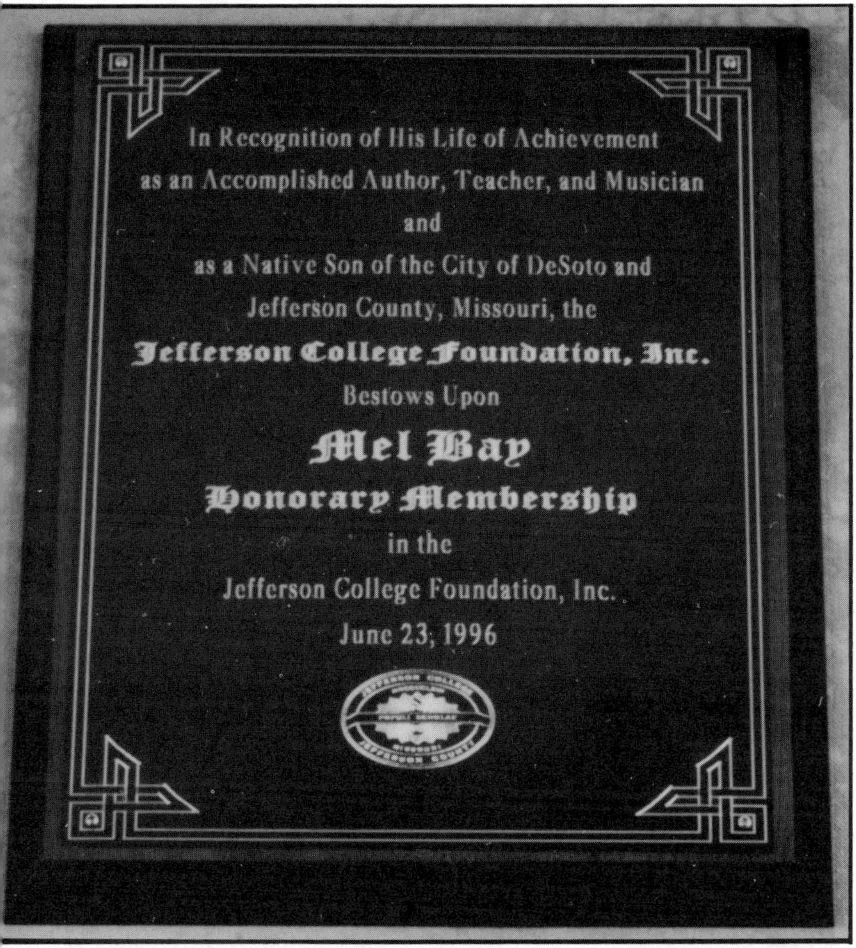

In Recognition of His Life of Achievement
as an Accomplished Author, Teacher, and Musician
and
as a Native Son of the City of DeSoto and
Jefferson County, Missouri, the
**Jefferson College Foundation, Inc.**
Bestows Upon
**Mel Bay**
**Honorary Membership**
in the
Jefferson College Foundation, Inc.
June 23, 1996

*On June 23, 1996 the Jefferson College Foundation, Inc. made Mel Bay an honorary member in recognition of "his Life of Achievement,"*

*This merit award was presented to Mel Bay for outstanding service to music educators.*

*Dick Renna, president of the American Federation of Musicians Local 2-197 presenting Mel (above) with the Owen Miller Lifetime Achievement Award for "Loyalty... Dedication... Fellowship and Fairness" towards members of the association.*

*The DeSoto National Education Association presented Mel with a "Distinguished Alumnus Award" in June of 1993.*

***"Successful teaching is hard work and requires much planning, but the rewards are well worth it."***

**– Mel Bay**

*A long-time Rotary member who has attended meetings around the world, Mel Bay receives a special recognition award from his hometown chapter in DeSoto, Missouri.*

*This award was presented to Mel by the Kirkwood Chamber of Commerce, naming him the Small Business Person of the Year in 1986.*

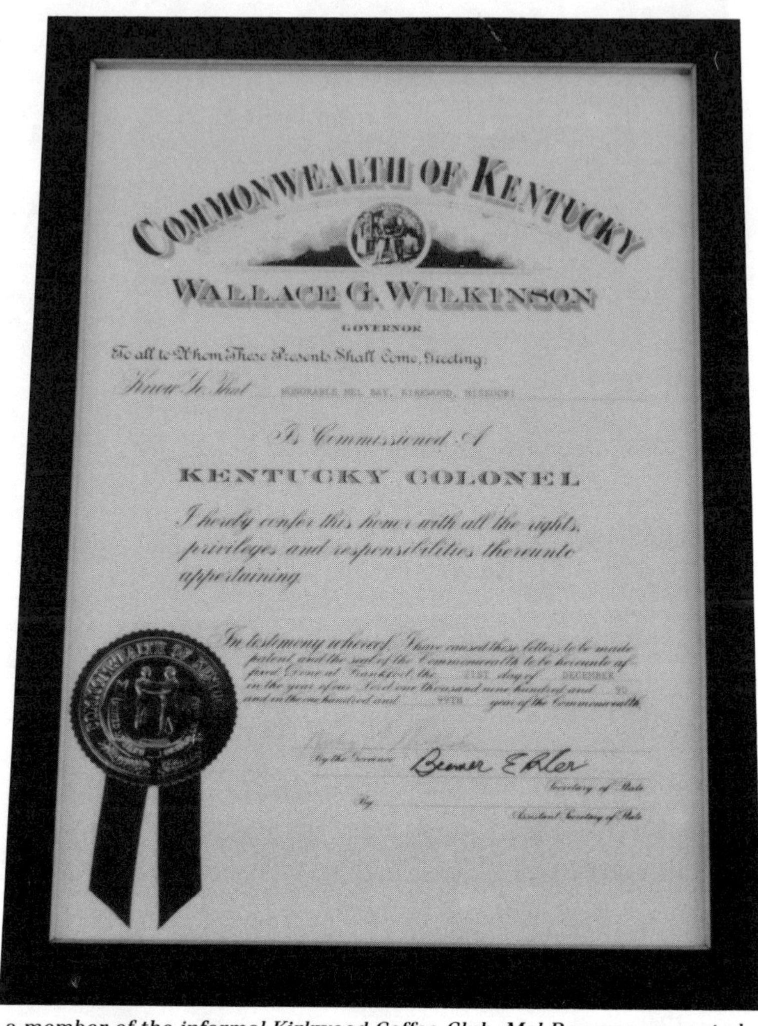

COMMONWEALTH OF KENTUCKY

WALLACE G. WILKINSON

GOVERNOR

To all to Whom These Presents Shall Come, Greeting:

Know Ye That

Is Commissioned A

KENTUCKY COLONEL

I hereby confer this honor with all the rights, privileges and responsibilities thereunto appertaining.

*As a member of the informal Kirkwood Coffee Club, Mel Bay was presented with this Kentucky Colonel plaque. The presentation was made at the Kirkwood City Hall by Mayor Herb Jones and club member Ben Thompson.*

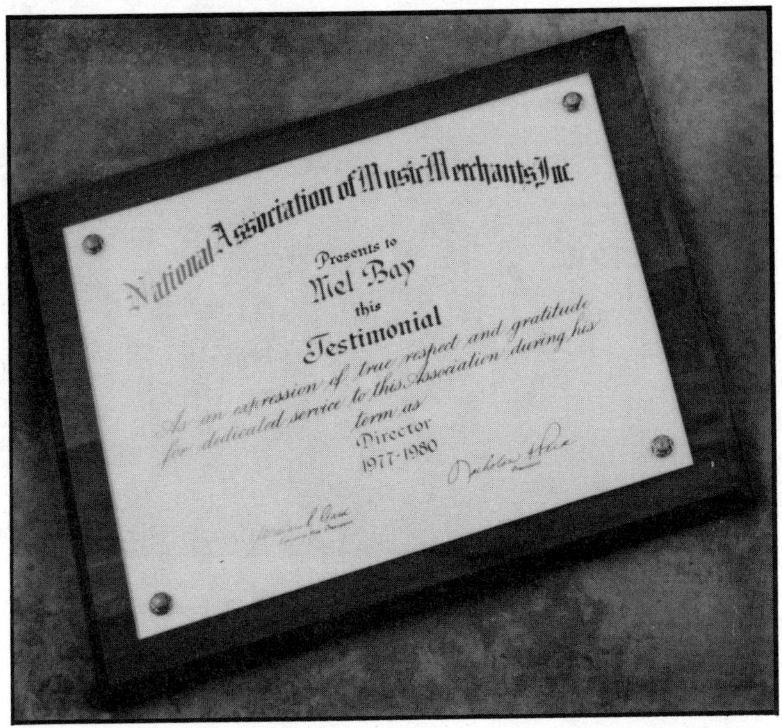


*The National Association of Music Merchants presented the testimonial to Mel Bay to express "respect and gratitude for dedicated service to the Association during his term as Director" from 1977-1980.*

***"A person is going to pick up the instruction book, look through it and ask: 'Do I understand this?' You've got to put yourself in the part of the player."***

**– Mel Bay**

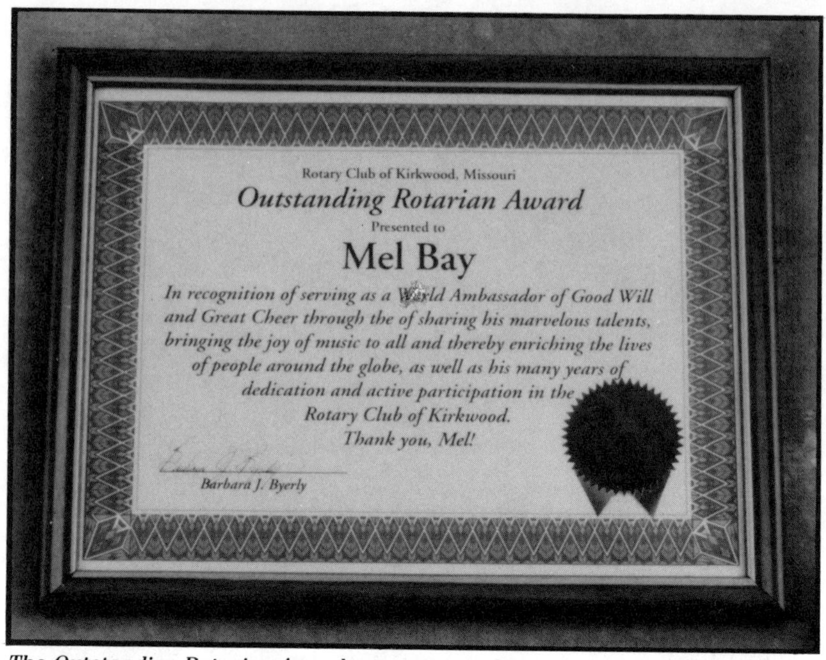


*The Outstanding Rotarian Award was presented to Mel for being "a World Ambassador of Good Will and Good Cheer" by the Rotary Club of Kirkwood, Missouri.*

***"A lot of writers are on ego trips. They write a book as a kind of monument to their ego. The thing that used to chagrin the life out of me was when a writer would take a lot of my time telling he about how good he was, about his great background, and so on.***

***"The public doesn't care about that stuff. People are interested in what the book is going to do for them. I don't care how great a background you have – if the book doesn't fill a need, it won't sell."***

**– Mel Bay**

Mel Bay and renowned trumpet teacher Ed Brauer (Bill's trumpet teacher).

The Certificate of Merit presented to Mel Bay by the St. Louis Suburban Music Education Association.

*Elmer Herrick presenting Mel with the American Guild of Music's Outstanding Achievement Award (above).*

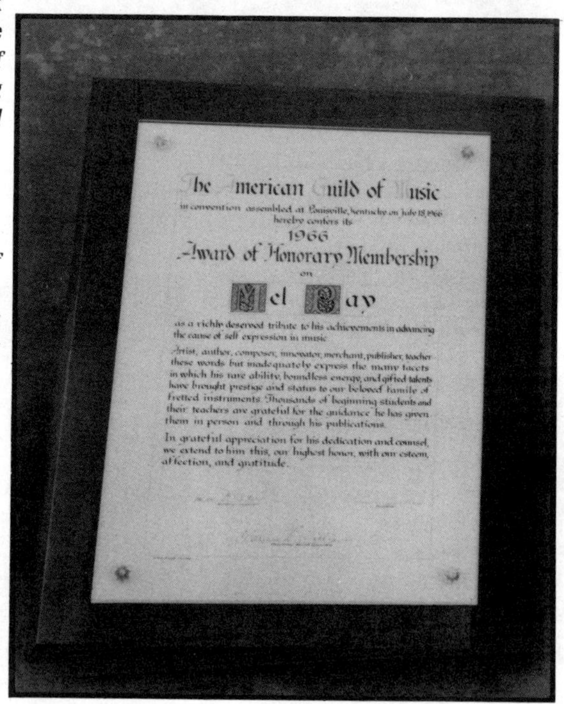

The American Guild of Music
in convention assembled at Louisville, Kentucky on July 18, 1966
hereby confers its
1966
Award of Honorary Membership
on
Mel Bay
as a richly deserved tribute to his achievements in advancing the cause of self expression in music.

Artist, author, composer, innovator, merchant, publisher, teacher these words but inadequately express the many facets in which his rare ability, boundless energy, and gifted talents have brought prestige and status to our beloved family of fretted instruments. Thousands of beginning students and their teachers are grateful for the guidance he has given them in person and through his publications.

In grateful appreciation for his dedication and counsel, we extend to him this, our highest honor, with our esteem, affection, and gratitude.

*The American Guild of Music made Mel Bay an honorary member (right) for "advancing the cause of self-expression in music."*

# Mel's Many Friends

As Johnny Smith said in his introduction to this book, Mel Bay is a very wealthy man in terms of friends. Mel thrives on talking to an endless stream of friends – in the store, on the street, on the phone, wherever he is. On the following pages are photos of just a few of his many friends...

*The inscription on this photo from Chet Atkins reads: "To my dear friend, Mel Bay, who taught the world."*

*John Becker, Roy Clark, and Mel Bay*

*Mel and Roy Smeck*

*Long-time friend John Becker (above) has traveled the world playing tenor banjo and now plays with Mel Bay and Stan Musial at special events.*

*Mel and Johnny Smith enjoying some trout fishing together (left).*

*Mel Bay says: "One Friday night when I was a young boy I turned the radio on and heard the most beautiful tenor banjo played by Harry Reser. His rendition of 'Lollypops' really hooked me! From that time on I glued my ears to the Atwater-Kent radio, listening to the Cliquot Club Eskimos led by this great musician. I eventually memorized every solo published by him."*

*Charlie Menees, a well-known St. Louis radio personality and jazz music historian, and a good friend of Mel Bay.*

*Menees said that he wanted to be a musician, but since he didn't feel that he had the talent, he spent a large part of his lifetime becoming a friend of many of the great musicians – Duke Ellington, Woody Herman, Pete Fountain, and dozens of other recognizable names during the great jazz period from the 1930s up to the 1950s.*

*Menees hosted "Big Band Bash" and "Jazz Freeway" on St. Louis radio stations.*

*He had a record collection of more than 25,000 albums, which his widow Mary Kay donated to The University of Missouri in Kansas City.*

*Charlie's radio nickname was "Cactus Charlie" bestowed on him by a radio staffer after Charlie and Mary Kay came back from a 1973 visit to Arizona and Charlie proclaimed that the weather there was "so kind" to his life-long bone diseases.*

*Charlie died in 1993 after suffering a heart attack while doing one of his Saturday night four-hour jazz programs.*

*His funeral at the big First Presbyterian Church in Kirkwood was climaxed by the Gateway City Big Band of some 30 members "blowing the roof off the church," as Charlie would have liked it.*

*Mel with jazz radio host Charlie Menees and legendary jazz guitarist George Van Eps.*

*Mel with Johnny Smith and famed guitar maker Jimmy D'Aguisto.*

*Mel Bay with Roger Filiberto, a music teacher in New Orleans. Filiberto wrote an electric bass method book which sold more than a million copies.*

## *An Air Force general pays Mel a tribute*

Young U.S. Air Corps pilot Bob Buechler was sitting on a sandbag at an air base in Upper Assam (Bangladesh) in 1943, in the early days of World War II. He was waiting for orders to get into a B-25 bomber and fly out on a mission over Rangoon against the Japanese. There was nothing to do but sit, and wait, because the target was socked in by bad flying weather. It was hot, and it was boring for a young pilot, itchy to jump into that plane and do what he had to do.

One of Buechler's squadron members was sitting on a sandbag near him, strumming a guitar, just to pass the time.

Buechler watched and listened. Finally, out of sheer boredom, he asked: "Do you mind if I try that?"

His buddy obliged, and handed over the guitar.

Buechler held it awkwardly and ran his thumb over the strings.

Today, more than 50 years later, he laughs and says: "At that moment, I was hooked!"

Today, Buechler is still hooked on guitars, and is quick to pick up his Johnny Smith Heritage and show off his fondness of playing it. Through the more than 50 years since picking up that first guitar at the air base, Buechler has owned and traded several guitars, including a Gibson 400 that he bought from a dealer in Spokane, Washington.

One of his many moves around the world brought Buechler back to St. Louis, Missouri – his original hometown. His continuing pursuit of guitars and guitar accessories took him into the Mel Bay Music Center in Kirkwood, a St. Louis suburb.

"My good fortune," he says now, "was to be waited on by Mr. Mel Bay himself!

"We struck up a conversation, which has been followed by many other conversations, and luncheons, and other get-togethers," Buechler says.

"I have been out to Mel Bay's retreat in Colorado – we have spent a lot of time together. Mel introduced me to the great Johnny Smith, who lives in Colorado Springs, and that's why I am so proud to own one of his guitars," Buechler adds.

During his 36 years of service, today's Major General Bob Buechler (U.S. Air Force, Retired) has been all over the world and met many high-ranking and well-known people. During his first stint in World War II Buechler was the personal pilot for Lord Mountbatten, the Supreme Allied Commander of all Armed Forces in the Asian Theatre. He has known U.S. Presidents, foreign heads of state including Chiang Kai Shek and Mao Tse Tung, military greats like Gen. Claire Chennault, General Stratemeyer, and General Joe Stilwell, movie stars, corporate executives, and even a current prince in Saudi Arabia, with whom he flies to Africa in his private plane.

But, when he sifts through the years, and the countless names and memories, Bob Buechler unabashedly has this to say about Mel Bay:

"He is one of the most unique and admirable people that I have ever met.

"He believes in old-fashioned character values.

"He is thoughtful, and has a great sense of humor.

"He is learned and articulate, and an astute businessman.

"He is considerate, fair, and sensitive. He is a workaholic, which has bred him great success."

*Major General Bob Buechler (U.S. Air Force, Retired) had this to say on his signed photo: "To Mel Bay, The best of the best. My friend & confidant - Bob Buechler."*

# Geriatric Jazz

*A special plaque awarded to the "Geriatric Jazz" group, consisting of Mel Bay and John Becker on banjos, and baseball Hall of Famer Stan Musial on harmonica.*

*Baseball Hall of Famer Stan Musial and Mel Bay, plus John Becker shown in back between them, are regular performers at many events including an annual fall Jamboree in front of the Mel Bay Music Center in Kirkwood, Missouri. Mel and John play banjos – sometimes Mel plays guitar – and Stan plays harmonica.*

*Performing here at the Kirkwood, Missouri fall jamboree, John Becker, world-renowned banjoist, Mel Bay, who can switch easily from one stringed instrument to another, and Stan Musial, baseball Hall of Famer and harmonica player, always draw a large and appreciative audience.*

*John Becker, Mel Bay, and Stan Musial, perform together as "Geriatric Jazz."*

*Roy Smeck, the "Wizard of the Strings" who befriended young Mel Bay in 1927, later joined up with Mel, now an accomplished guitarist, to do special performances (above). Note: Ed Shaughnessy is the drummer.*

*Mel with pianist/ composer Matt Dennis and Matt's wife, renowned singer Ginny Dennis.*

# Letters to Mel Bay

*Mel Bay gets letters from around the world*

As Mel Bay's guitar instruction books began moving into wider and wider distribution around the world, letters began to trickle in to Mel.

First a trickle, then almost a steady flow, and it continues.

Where do the letters come from, and who writes them? They come, literally, from all over the globe.

And they are written by people who have been touched in some way by Mel Bay books.

They come from people in all walks of life – doctors, preachers, scientists, professors, farmers, travelers, even a prisoner on death row.

All send along the same basic thought – "thanks to Mel Bay for writing those great books so that I – or my friend – could learn to play the guitar!"

Mel Bay says: "The letters that we receive are one of the great satisfactions we get for the work we have done."

Following is a small sampling of some of the letters that have come in to Mel Bay personally, and to the Mel Bay Publishing Company...

Institution *Florida State Prison*
Name *Mack Tedder Jr.*
Job Assignment *Death Row*

Cell Number *182108*
Number *035639*
Date *Nov. 2, 1975*

*Dear Mr. Bay:*

*I am with the ambition of learning to play the guitar, but I'll have to teach myself as I'm on Death Row. Do you know of any cheap publications that could teach me, as I'm very limited on funds.*

*At a very early age, I learnt enough about a guitar to play several songs, til I lost my guitar. I used a pick then, and I'd like to use one now. I have forgotten all I had previously learned, except a couple of chords.*

*Thank you very much for your time!*

*Awaiting your reply – I remain*
*Sincerely yours,*

(signed) *Mack Tedder Jr.*

*P.S. I am also interested in a good cheap Harmonica learning book.*

(on the original letter is Mel Bay's handwriting: "books sent 11/6")

INSTITUTION Florida State Prison CELL NUMBER 182108

NAME Mack Tedder Jr NUMBER 035639

JOB ASSIGNMENT Death Row DATE Nov. 2, 1975

Dear Mr. Bay,

I am with the ambition of learning to play the guitar, but I'll have to teach myself as I'm on Death Row. Do you know of any cheap publications that could teach me, as I'm very limited on funds. At a very early age, I learnt enough about a guitar to play several songs, til I lost my guitar. I used a pick then, and I'd like to use one now. I have forgotten all I had previously learned, except a couple of Cords.

Thank you very much for your time! awaiting your reply - I remain

Sincerely your's,

Mack Tedder Jr
182108-035639
P.O. Box 747
Starke, FL. 32091

books sent 11/6

P.S. I am also interested in a good cheap Harmonica learning book.

MACK TEDDER Jr
[illegible]

BEFORE CORRESPONDING PLEASE READ RULES ON REVERSE SIDE

A dentist in Milwaukee writes Mel a letter about his travels...

*22 July, 1996*

*Mel,*

*I just returned from 2 weeks on the Island of Moorea in French Polynesia...Your books, as your fame, spread very far on this small planet.*

*Have you ever thought of doing a book on island songs?*

*All the best,*
*Your friend back in Wisconsin*

(signed) *John Masel*

## From Acapulco, Mexico, April 27, 1980...

Acapulco, Gro. April 27, 1980

Mr. Mel Bay
Pacific, Mo 63069

Dear Mr. Bay:

The most exciting surprise in my life was when I received your magnificent parcel post envolving the music material you were so kind to send me. I am very obliged to you and say THANKS to cover my duty entirely.

Immediately I put to work fingers and add to my programs the "Impressionist Period Music" material. Very clean fingering and excellent transcriptions.

I proudly exhibit your autographic memo to executives of Las Brisas, they compliment me for it. Besides, the Syndicate of musicians here in Acapulco took note of your business address for ordering the material announced in your catalog.

Now with new strings and music I have the purpose to make cassettes or records and send to you as a souvenir and a way of expression of my compliments to you.

I left for final this reflection: "How was it possible not know that you and friends were dining at The Arsenal?" Please excuse me this fault but I don't imagine it. From my youth I remember some of your editions of jazz. I played sometimes banjo tenor in small groups for dancing and shows in Mexico City.

Thank you again, Mr. Bay.

(signed) Guillermo Torres S.

# A letter from Quebec, Canada...

ÉCOLE SECONDAIRE CLASSIQUE
CONGRÉGATION DE NOTRE-DAME
393, DE LANAUDIÈRE, JOLIETTE

February 18, 1972

Mel Bay Publications Inc.
107 West Jefferson Avenue
Kirkwood, Missouri, 63122

Dear Sir:

I have just received the two Volumes that you so kindly sent me and I wish to convey my sincere appreciation and gratitude to you for this precious gift.

I do not have the privilege of knowing you personally, but from what I can judge from your works, you must be a wonderful music player and teacher. You have such a way of explaining things most clearly in a few words and of presenting new notions that is very encouraging and stimulating. It is a real pleasure to learn the Guitar with your excellent Method which is based on pedagogy and experience.

I have shown the catalog of your publications to some of my friends and they have been greatly interested.

May God bless you and all your undertakings !

Yours thankfully,

Sr Yvonne Hétu, c.n.d.

Sr Yvonne Hétu, C.N.D.
393, De Lanaudière St.
Joliette, P. Québec, Canada

A letter from Russia – in 1963 while under communist rule – from a professor of guitar...

*Professeur de Guitare*
*Arsene V. Popov*
*per. Plekhanova 24*
*Tomsk, U.R.S.S.*

*Tomsk, 15/XII/63*

*Dear Sir:*

*Thank you for your most welcome letter dated 13/XI/63 and for your catalogue of guitar music.*

*It was a great pleasure to read your letter, to know of your interest and activities. You can be sure I am very interested in an exchange of materials.*

*I am of the opinion that the pedagogy of the instrument has not been well enough thought through on the basis of contemporary thinking and I would be interested therefore in your publications.*

*I am sending to you, by sea mail post registered, my first parcel of music for classic guitar published in our country amounting to the value of $9.00.*

*For my part I would be more than obliged if you could possibly send me the following, your publications:*

*1) Mel Bay Graded Classic Guitar Method;*

*2) Mel Bay Folio of Classic Guitar Solos edited by Joseph Castle.*

(signed) *A. Popov*

Here's a letter from Turkey...

*4th of July, 1965*

*Dear Sir,*

*I had written and asked you to send me some books of "Mel Bay." I got the books a few days ago.*

*I want to thank you because of your courtesy. It was such a kind act that I'll never forget.*

*I also want to help you as much as I can.*

*If you need anything from Turkey, please make me know it. I'll do my best to help you.*

(signed) *Ijlku Tinel*
*Sumerbank Iplih Fabrikasi*
*Sosyal Hiemetler sef. eglu*
*Denizli, Turkey*

A letter from Yugoslavia (no date, but Mel Bay thinks it was in the 1960s)...

*To: Mel Bay Publications*

*I have read in American library in Zagreb that Mel Bay Publications is one of the best publishers of guitar music in USA.*

*I am young guitarist and I have learned all basic guitar chords.*

*Now I should like to start solo guitar, but I have no literature for it.*

*Because of this, I beg you to be so kind and send me some book of guitar solos for teaching.*

*Something for advanced students.*

*Excuse me for this, my wish.*

*Yours sincerely,*

(signed) *Zivkovic Drago*
*SRB, LIKA*
*YUGOSLAVIA*

Here is a letter from an Italian guitarist in Sweden...

*Stockholm, 2/2/65*

*Dear Mr. Mel Bay:*

*I am an Italian guitar player working actually here in Scandinavia, and of course, reading about your "Method For the Modern Guitar." I am very interested in it.*

*Would you please be so kind to inform me if this method (I mean, all 7 graded books) is still available, and eventually, how many dollars should I send to get it here in Sweden.*

*Please, answer me as soon as possible in the way I can order it.*

*Thank you very much for the attention and excuse my bad English.*

*Hope you'll understand me!!*

*Yours,*

(signed) *Claudio Marussi*

*P.S. Just now I have finished "to master out your CHORD SYSTEM FOR THE ORCHESTRAL GUITAR."*

*Really, atomic power in every chord!*

*I have found here in Stockholm 2 books: "World famous Songs for Guitar," and "Play Guitar Like Mel Bay." There are other publications?*

(Mel wrote these instructions on this letter: "Send Airmail Jazz II.")

One letter to Mel Bay was addressed to no street address, and to the wrong state – Montana!

It still reached Mel Bay.

As you can see by this photo, it came from Iran, and it was addressed:

To: Mel Bay Publications
Kirkwood, Montana
<u>U.S.A.</u>

(Maybe somebody in the U.S. Postal system had learned to play from a Mel Bay book and knew how to direct the letter?)

*This letter to Mel Bay from an admirer in Iran was addressed to Kirkwood, MONTANA...but it still managed to make its way to Mel.*

A letter from the "Wizard of the Strings"...

ROY SMECK
WIZARD OF STRINGS
STAGE SCREEN T.V.
AND RECORDING ARTIST

590 WEST END AVENUE
NEW YORK, NEW YORK 10024
TRAFALGAR 4-7636

Dear Pal Mel
the Best

Sunday
June 27th
1982

First thanks for the Strings and DOUBLE thanks FOR Comeing to New YORK to Be in MY Movie - AFter 54 YEARS - YOU PLAYED the Guitar Better then ever - AND Better than ever My FRIEND it would Be A great thing IF YOU AND I DID A CONCERT

(2)

to goather Be For its to Late
You CAN PLAy the Banjos
to goather - Guitar with the
Uke And two Guitars And Haw
Guitar with you on the Guitar
And I Now Have 4 Noveltios on
the Uke And 2 hr's I Do in the
Concert's OK - the time went
So Fast - I will take the New
ALBUM to Miss Damdell -
Hope to hear From you take
Care - Fay And I Send Are Love
to ALL And the Best to you your Uke
PAL Roy

A letter from a retired distributor, dated 5/16/91

5/16/91

Dear Mel

I Know This Letter will come as a Pleasant surprise to you as it Has Been years since I had any contact with you personally. But looking at your picture surrounded by your Son + 6 Grandsons gave me the urge to drop you a note.

We sold our business in 1980 and being that my wife Frances was born + raised in Louisiana she talked me into retirement. + of course Louisiana where we would be close to her family. We settled herein 1988. My name Syd Heller Studio is still on your mailing list + I enjoy getting circulars. And of course brings back wonderful memories of you + how you really started me in selling music books in a big way.

I realy don't remember the year you walked into our store + noticed

A SMALL RACK OF MUSIC BOOKS, CLOSE TO THE ENTRANCE. AFTER TALKING to ME ONLY A FEW MINUTES ABOUT PROFITS + DEMAND. YOU CONVINCED ME AND LIT THE SPARK THAT WAS to MAKE OUR STORE THE LARGEST MEL BAY MUSIC RETAILER IN SAN FRANCISCO. WE SOLD THEM to GUITAR TEACHERS PRISON INMATES, THE ARMED SERVICE'S, + OF COURSE OUR GREAT WALK IN TRADE. + ALL YOU SAID WAS THAT DISPLAY'S WERE THE KEY. SO WE HAD RACKS ALL OVER THE STORE + YOU KNOW OUR STORE WAS BIG 4,600 FT. + YOU WERE RIGHT MEL OUR MUSIC BOOK BUSINESS TOOK OFF LIKE FIRE + THAT DEPT WAS VERY PROFITABLE. SO I JUST WANT to SAY THANK YOU to A MAN WHO NOT ONLY HAD VISION, BUT WAS A PERSONAL FRIEND TO ALL HIS CUSTOMERS + DEALERS. GOD BLESS YOU - YOUR WONDERFUL FAMILY + THE MEL BAY ORGANIZATION.

SINCERELY Syd Heller COLUMBIA MUSI Co

OVER

THE WHITE HOUSE

WASHINGTON

October 18, 1996

Warm greetings to everyone gathered in St. Louis, Missouri, for the 1996 Guitar Foundation of America International Festival and Guitar Competition. I am pleased to join you in honoring the extraordinary contributions of Chet Atkins, Mel Bay, and Aaron Shearer to our nation.

Enriching many musical traditions -- from classical to folk, from country to jazz to blues-- the guitar holds a unique place in our cultural heritage. Through its versatility and powerful resonance, the guitar conveys a wide range of emotions, paints vivid pictures of human experience, and reinforces the bonds that link all of us together.

This festival provides you a wonderful opportunity to share your love of guitar, to study with master guitarists, and to develop lasting international friendships. I salute the participants for their proven dedication to excellence and musicianship, and I commend the organizers and supporters for encouraging the growth of young artists.

Best wishes for a memorable festival and an exciting competition.

Bill Clinton

LEROY ANDERSON
WOODBURY, CONNECTICUT

June 8, 1961

Mr. Mel Bay
133 West Jefferson Avenue
Kirkwood 22, Missouri

Dear Mr. Bay:

Thank you for making the changes in the folio of my music. I checked the proofs before it went to print and noticed that you made a number of other corrections and improvements.

I appreciate your painstaking work and hope that you will be able to do more arrangements of my music.

With best regards, I am,

Sincerely,

Leroy Anderson

AMERICAN MUSIC CONFERENCE

332 South Michigan Avenue • CHICAGO 4 • Telephone HArrison 7-9492

October 6, 1960

Mr. Mel Bay
Mel Bay Studios
Kirkwood
Missouri

Dear Mel:

Many, many thanks for the fine job that you did in demonstrating the guitar at the National Recreation Congress in Washington, D. C. on September 28th. I believe that it was self evident to you that the audience profited a great deal by what you had to show them. Their response was as I should expect it to be.

It is always nice to be working with you, and I thank you for your help at this meeting.

My congratualtions to you on the fine demonstration that you gave.

Sincerely,

(Mr.) Marion S. Egbert
Vice-President, Head
Consultant Services

MSE/t
cc: J. Kraus

**Northeast Missouri State University** **NMSU**
**Kirksville, Missouri 63501** **Phone 816 665-5121**

July 9, 1975

Mr. Mel Bay
The Mel Bay Music Center
107 W. Jefferson
St. Louis, Missouri 63122

Dear Mr. Bay:

Let me try to express our collective thanks for the workshop you presented here two weeks ago, for the materials you made available to the students and to us, and for the most pleasant association we enjoyed with you while you were here.

The workshop achieved all that could be done with the time span you had to work and the students all seem to be most appreciative of what you gave them. I hope the time may come when you might be able to come back and conduct an intermediate workshop for some we have who are now anxious to move on a little! If we are able to add a guitar class to our regular curriculum this year or next, I will certainly let you know.

My wife and I enjoyed very much the little time we were able to spend with you and appreciate your sending the Get-Away brochure. It appears that we will be postponing our trip until spring but strangely I don't feel disappointed so long as we can do it then. The dollar picked up a little the last day or so; maybe it will continue.

I hope we will enjoy the opportunity to visit with you again. Please accept our heartiest thanks for your contribution to our summer program!

Sincerely,

Dale

Dale A. Jorgenson
Head, Division of Fine Arts

DAJ:ge
Enc.

Theodore Presser Co.

*MUSIC PUBLISHERS SINCE 1783*

July 1, 1996

Mr. Mel Bay, Founder
Mel Bay Publications, Inc.
4 Dailey Industrial Park
Pacific, MO 63069

Dear Mr. Bay:

It was a genuine thrill to meet you in St. Louis during the RPMDA convention. The word "legend" has become one that is used too frequently these days, but in your case the word is entirely appropriate. You are not only a legend in the music making field but also in the music publishing field. I have been hearing "Mel Bay stories" for much of my life.

I was touched that you took the time to tell me about your first book on guitar playing, the CARCASSI METHOD FOR THE GUITAR. When you told me that you still have your original copy from the 1920s, I became concerned that it might not be in top condition, so I have enclosed a brand new copy with our compliments. I hasten to add that I do not wish to imply that you need any further instruction but if you feel the need to brush up on your technique, you should have a crisp copy of the Carcassi book. On the other hand, you have several wonderful books of your own!

I hope I have another opportunity to talk with you about the music business in the near future.

Best regards,

Thomas Broido
President

TB/ea

*1 Presser Place, Bryn Mawr, Pennsylvania 19010-3490*
*FAX (610) 527-7841* *(610) 525-3636*

**Retail Print Music Dealers Association**

4020 McEwen, Suite 105 • Dallas, Texas 75244-5019 • 214/233-9107 • Fax 214/490-4219

President
Michael S. Sagun
Sheet Music Service of Portland
34 NW 8th Avenue
Portland, OR 97209
503/222-9607
Fax 503/222-9600

Vice President/Secretary
Richard Gore
Pender's Music Co.
314 South Elm
Denton, TX 76201
817/382-7124
Fax 817/382-0869

Vice President/Treasurer
Laurie Austin
Heid Music, Inc.
308 E. College Ave.
Appleton, WI 54911
414/734-1969
Fax 414/734-2164

Past President
Ed Walker
Baxter-Northup Music Co.
14534 Ventura Blvd.
Sherman Oaks, CA 91403
818/788-7510
Fax 818/986-1297

Member at Large
Ken Anderson
Flesher-Hinton Music Co.
3936 Tennyson ST.
Denver, CO 80212
303/433-8891
Fax 303/455-7062

Member at Large
Anna Marie Mannerino
7605 Hamilton Ave.
Cincinnati, OH 45231
513/522-8975
Fax 513/522-8991

Associate Member at Large
Bill Heese
Carl Fischer, Inc.
62 Cooper Square
NewYork, NY 10003
212/777-0900
Fax 212/477-4129

RPMDA Headquarters
4020 McEwen #105
Dallas, TX 75244-5019
214/233-9107
Fax 214/490-4219

Mel Bay
Mel Bay Publications, Inc
#4 Industrial Dr.
Pacific, MO 63069

June 6, 1996

Dear Mel :

Bravo! for your wonderful performance. The entire audience was spellbound by the entire evening. We shall never forget the magical experience and the happiness you have shared with all of us.

I appreciate your planning and preparation which helped make the evening a success. It is exciting to know people have the opportunity to learn both music and life skills from you. You are truly a marvelous person and I wish you much success and happiness.

Thank you for sharing your time and talents with us during our convention. You have made our 20th Anniversary Convention Gala a very special event.

Sincerely,

Richard Gore

Richard Gore
Program Chairman, St. Louis '96

# Some Facts and Figures

*How Mel's books stack up*

Mel Bay has sold more than 20 million of his standard type guitar books.

If you stacked those up (1/8th inch per book) you would have a *stack 40 miles high!*

– Or –

If you laid 20 million books end to end, they would stretch from coast to coast across the United States, and from the Canadian border down to the Gulf of Mexico!

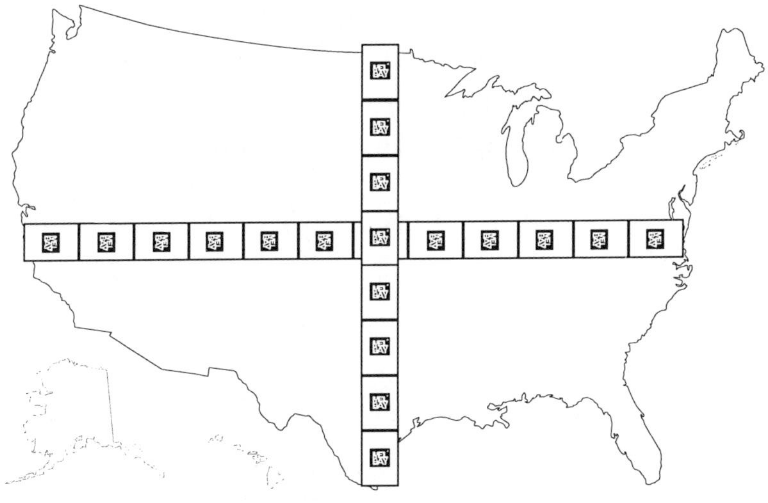

# A Special Honor

*The week of October 20, 1996, was a big one for the city of St. Louis, and for Mel Bay and his family. Here are a few highlights...*

The annual Guitar Foundation of America International Conference was held at Webster University in St. Louis October 21-26. Hundreds of guitarists from across the United States and many European nations attended daily presentations, recitals, and concerts by world-class players as well as an eclectic vendors fair.

Highlights of the week included the young artist competition and the presentation of the GFA's Lifetime Achievement

Award to Chet Atkins, Mel Bay, and Aaron Shearer – each of whom was honored with a gala evening concert, a commemorative plaque, and a surprise proclamation from President Clinton. The significance of seeing these three American innovators of the guitar on the same stage was not lost on this audience.

On Friday, October 25 Mel Bay was honored with a special concert featuring the Los Angeles Guitar Quartet, the father and son jazz guitar duo of Bucky and John Pizzarelli, and the Strano sisters duo presenting the world premier of Andrew York's double guitar concerto entitled *Word.* It would be hard to imagine a concert with a more infectious, electrifying rapport between players and audience. All three segments of the concert were met with standing ovations which in turn were

*1996 GFA Convention director John McClellan (left) and assistant present Mel Bay with a mayoral proclamation.*

rewarded with encores. Before the intermission, jazz guitar giant Johnny Smith paid a moving, yet humorous tribute to Mel Bay.

Conference director John McClellan presented Mr. Bay with the GFA's Lifetime Achievement Award which read:

> 1996 GFA International Convention
> and Competition
> The Guitar Foundation of America presents this
> Lifetime Achievement Award
> to Mel Bay,
> publisher, arranger, and guitarist
> whose methods have influenced
> millions of guitarists throughout the world.
> October 25, 1996

In additional, Mr. McClellan presented Mr. Bay with a hand-lettered, framed mayoral proclamation which read as follows:

> WHEREAS
>
> Mel Bay has made a significant contribution to music education in America and around the globe, establishing Mel Bay Publications, Inc., now celebrating its 50th anniversary as one of the world's largest independent music publishers, and a leading publisher of music for guitar and other fretted instruments.
>
> In addition to being a pioneer and innovator in creating a modern guitar repertoire and teaching method, Mel has worked tirelessly as a music educator, performer, composer, arranger, and merchant, providing quality services and instruments for the St. Louis community and touching thousands of lives with the gift of music.
>
> Now, therefore, I, Freeman R. Bosley, Jr., Mayor of the City of St. Louis, do hereby proclaim October 25, 1996, as Mel Bay Day.

The performance was followed by a reception for the evening's performers and Mr. Bay's family and friends.

*The Guitar Foundation of America presented this Lifetime Achievement Award to Mel Bay on October 25, 1996.*

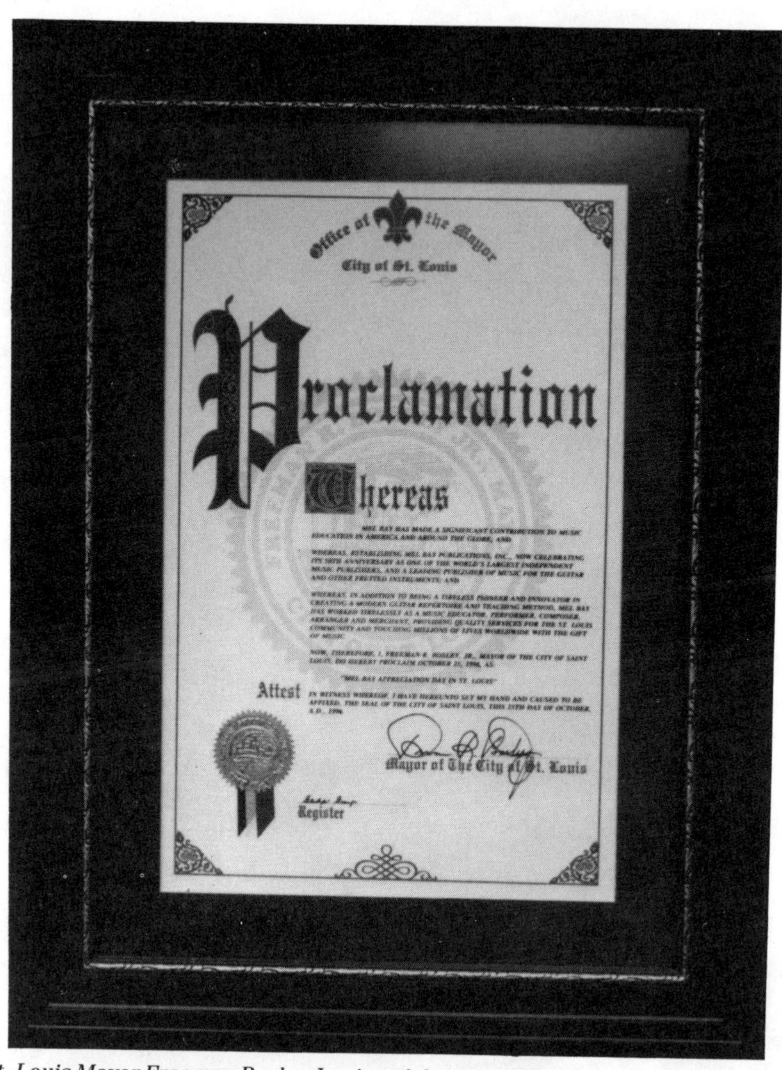

Office of the Mayor
City of St. Louis

Proclamation

Whereas

MEL BAY HAS MADE A SIGNIFICANT CONTRIBUTION TO MUSIC EDUCATION IN AMERICA AND AROUND THE GLOBE; AND

WHEREAS, ESTABLISHING MEL BAY PUBLICATIONS, INC., NOW CELEBRATING ITS 50TH ANNIVERSARY AS ONE OF THE WORLD'S LARGEST INDEPENDENT MUSIC PUBLISHERS, AND A LEADING PUBLISHER OF MUSIC FOR THE GUITAR AND OTHER FRETTED INSTRUMENTS; AND

WHEREAS, IN ADDITION TO BEING A TIRELESS PIONEER AND INNOVATOR IN CREATING A MODERN GUITAR REPERTOIRE AND TEACHING METHOD, MEL BAY HAS WORKED TIRELESSLY AS A MUSIC EDUCATOR, PERFORMER, COMPOSER, ARRANGER AND MERCHANT, PROVIDING QUALITY SERVICES FOR THE ST. LOUIS COMMUNITY AND TOUCHING MILLIONS OF LIVES WORLDWIDE WITH THE GIFT OF MUSIC.

NOW, THEREFORE, I, FREEMAN R. BOSLEY, JR., MAYOR OF THE CITY OF SAINT LOUIS, DO HEREBY PROCLAIM OCTOBER 25, 1996, AS

"MEL BAY APPRECIATION DAY IN ST. LOUIS"

Attest

IN WITNESS WHEREOF, I HAVE HEREUNTO SET MY HAND AND CAUSED TO BE AFFIXED, THE SEAL OF THE CITY OF SAINT LOUIS, THIS 25TH DAY OF OCTOBER, A.D., 1996.

Mayor of The City of St. Louis

Register

*St. Louis Mayor Freeman Bosley Jr. signed the proclamation making October 25, 1996 "Mel Bay Appreciation Day In St. Louis."*

*John and Bucky Pizzarelli bring down the house.*

*York, Dearman, Tennant, Kanengiser – the Los Angeles Guitar Quartet!*

*The Strano sisters perform Andrew York's Word with the GFA orchestra.*

*These three renowned names in the guitar field were all honored during the big Guitar Foundation of America International Convention and Competition in October of 1996 in St. Louis – Mel Bay, Aaron Shearer, and Chet Atkins.*

*Johnny Smith, Mel and May Bay (above) look on from the front row during the festivities to honor Mel.*

*At left, Johnny Smith, Chet Atkins and William Bay at the Guitar Foundation of America convention.*

*Johnny Smith (above left), noted jazz guitarist who played for Bing Crosby and the NBC orchestra, and who made many of his own albums – and long-time friend of Mel Bay, pays a special tribute to Mel at the Sheldon Concert Hall in St. Louis on October 25, 1996.*

*John McClellan presents the GFA's "Lifetime Achievement Award" to Mel Bay.*

Missouri House of Representatives

**Resolution**

*Whereas*, the members of the Missouri House of Representatives welcome the opportunity to recognize a celebrated musician who has enriched the lives of countless others by sharing his considerable talent and knowledge as one of this nation's foremost guitarists; and

*Whereas*, Mr. Mel Bay of Kirkwood, Missouri, was recently honored with a special "Tribute to Mel Bay" sponsored by the Guitar Foundation of America at Sheldon Concert Hall, where top musicians from all over the country gathered to help commemorate "Mel Bay Day"; and

*Whereas*, born in the Ozark mountain town of Bunker, Missouri, in 1913, Mel Bay displayed an early interest and aptitude for playing the guitar and the tenor banjo, and subsequently pursued this activity until establishing himself as a recognized master of both instruments; and

*Whereas*, Mr. Bay has been a valued resident of Kirkwood since 1933, during which time he has brought considerable honor and recognition to the area through his accomplishments as a renowned music educator, performer, composer, arranger, and merchant; and

*Whereas*, Mel Bay is well known throughout St. Louis and around the globe as a pioneer and innovator in creating a modern guitar repertoire and teaching method, as the founder of Mel Bay Publications, Inc., which is now celebrating fifty years as one of the world's largest independent music publishers and a leading publisher of music for the guitar and other fretted instruments; and as the author of many popular instructional books, including The Mel Bay Modern Guitar Method; and

*Whereas*, Mr. Bay's many noteworthy accolades include the Lifetime Achievement Award from the American Guild of Music; election to the NAMM Board of Directors; selection to the Sherry Brenner Guitar Hall of Fame in Madrid, Spain; the Heritage Award from the Piedmont Guitar Society; the Owen Miller Award from the American Federation of Musicians for "A Lifetime of Achievement and Contribution to the World of Music"; and "Fewest Putts in a Golf Tournament" at Greenbriar Hills Country Club:

*Now, therefore, be it resolved* that we, the members of the Missouri House of Representatives, Eighty-eighth General Assembly, hereby join unanimously in commending and applauding Mel Bay at this proud moment of well-deserved recognition for his lifetime of achievement in the musical arts, and further extend to him our very best wishes as he continues to be an inspiration to those around him; and

*Be it further resolved* that the Chief Clerk of the Missouri House of Representatives be instructed to prepare a properly inscribed copy of this resolution for Mr. Mel Bay, as a measure of our esteem for him.

Offered by ____________________
Representative Michael R. Gibbons
District No. 94

I, Steve Gaw, Speaker of the House of Representatives, Eighty-eighth General Assembly, Second Regular Session, do certify that the above is a true and correct copy of House Resolution No. 2129, adopted November 7, 1996.

____________________
Steve Gaw, Speaker

"Salus Populi Suprema Lex Esto"

*This is a photo of a resolution passed by the Missouri House of Representatives, Eighty-eighth General Assembly, honoring Mel Bay for his many accolades and achievements.*

*Mel Bay*

## *Father and son compliment each other:*

William Bay says of his father: "Mel was a visionary who has done as much for the guitar as anyone."

Says Mel about his son: "Bill is an innovator who really expanded the company beyond what I ever expected."